Wrightslaw

Special Education
Legal Developments and Cases
2015

Peter W. D. Wright, Esq.

Pamela Darr Wright, MA, MSW

Harbor House Law Press, Inc.

Hartfield, Virginia 23071

Wrightslaw: Special Education Legal Developments and Cases 2015

By Peter W. D. Wright and Pamela Darr Wright

Library of Congress Cataloging-in-Publication Data

Wright, Peter W. D. and Pamela Darr Wright

Wrightslaw: Special Education Legal Developments and Cases 2015
p. cm.
ISBN 13: 978-1-892320-39-1
ISBN 10: 1-892320-39-8

1. Law — Special Education — United States. 2. Children with disabilities — Education — United States. 3. Special education — Parent Participation — United States. I. Title.

10 9 8 7 6 5 4 3 2 1

Printing History

Harbor House Law Press, Inc. issues new editions to keep our publications current. New editions include major revisions of text and/or changes. New printings include minor changes and corrections.

     First Edition   June 2016

Disclaimer

The purpose of this book is to educate. Although efforts have been made to ensure that the publication is accurate, there may be mistakes, typographical and in content. If you are dissatisfied with the book, please return it to the publisher for a full refund.

When You Use a Self-Help Law Book

Law is always changing. The information contained in this book may or may not reflect current legal developments. For legal advice, you should consult with an attorney.

Bulk Purchases

Harbor House Law Press books are available at a discount for bulk purchases, academic sales or textbook adoptions. For information, contact Harbor House Law Press, P. O. Box 480, Hartfield, VA 23071. Please provide the title of the book, ISBN number, quantity, how the book will be used, and date needed.

Toll Free Phone Orders: (877) LAW IDEA or (877) 529-4332.

Toll Free Fax Orders: (800) 863-5348.

Contents

Chapter 3. Decisions in IDEA Cases by Courts of Appeal........ 41

Chapter 4. Legal Research & Tutorial: Google Scholar 89

Index 97

Introduction

If you are the parent of a child with a disability, you represent your child's interests. To effectively advocate for your child, you need to be aware of recent legal developments and decisions that may affect your child's education.

If you work as a teacher, related service provider, or administrator, you may receive incorrect legal advice. You need to know about new developments in special education law.

If you are an attorney or advocate who assists children with disabilities and their families, you have an ethical responsibility to be current on cases and other legal issues.

We wrote *Wrightslaw: Special Education Legal Developments and Cases 2015* to make it easier for you to stay up-to-date on new developments and decisions. This book includes legal developments and key decisions from the Courts of Appeals in IDEA cases during 2015.

Why You Need This Book

Wrightslaw: Special Education Legal Developments and Cases 2015 is unique.

Unique? You bet!

In this book, you have special education legal news and developments, from jury trials and settlements in teacher abuse cases to legal pleadings in a case that may be decided by the Supreme Court.

In this book, you have all key decisions in special education cases from the Courts of Appeals and cases initiated and settled by the Department of Justice in 2015.

You have all "Dear Colleague" Policy and Guidance letters published by the Office of Special Education Programs (OSEP) and the Office of Special Education and Rehabilitation Services (OSERS). These Guidance letters are very useful when you need to educate school staff and administrators about their legal responsibilities.

You need *Wrightslaw: Special Education Legal Developments and Cases 2015* because you want to know -- or you **need** to know -- about exciting new developments in special education law.

Exciting? Yes, legal developments and cases can be exciting!

It's exciting when a Court of Appeals refuses to allow a special education director to use the cloak of "qualified immunity" after she retaliated against a father who advocated for his child by filing false child abuse complaints against him.

It's important for you to know that cases are being dismissed because parents failed to exhaust their administrative remedies (request a special education due process hearing) before filing suit in federal court.

In Chapter 2, you will see how this issue, known as "Exhaustion," affected the family of a child with a disability whose school refused to allow her service dog to accompany her in school. The parents have appealed an adverse Court of Appeals decision to the U.S. Supreme Court.

If you advocate for children with disabilities, including your own children, you need to know the answers to these questions.

Can a parent request an Independent Educational Evaluation (IEE) in an area that was not previously assessed by the school district? (See OSEP Letter to Debbie Baus, page 33)

What corrective actions can a State Department of Education order a school district to take after that district failed to provide a child with FAPE? (See OSEP Letter to Deaton, page 34)

Can a school district unilaterally amend a child's IEP during a resolution meeting and make the revised IEP the subject of the due process hearing? (See OSEP Letter to Cohen, page 36)

Although the Individuals with Disabilities Act (IDEA 2004) has not been revised and reauthorized since 2004, the law continues to evolve. As you read cases, letter opinions, and Dear Colleague letters in Special Education Legal Developments and Cases 2015, you will see how the law is changing.

Here are a few examples.

The U.S. Department of Education issued a Policy Paper that says annual IEP goals must be aligned with State academic content standards for the grade in which the child is enrolled. You need to read this Policy Letter with new requirements for IEPs published by the Office of Special Educations (OSEP) in November 2015. (see page 38)

Did you know that schools must notify parents of their right to ask the school to destroy their child's Personally Identifiable Information (PII) when it is no longer needed to provide educational services? Did you know that the school must destroy the PII at the parent's request? (see page 38)

Have you read the Settlement Agreement between the U.S. Attorney's Office and Detroit Public Schools that requires the public schools to provide sign language interpreters to parents who are deaf and hard of hearing so they can participate in educational decision-making? (see page 37)

How to Use This Book

Wrightslaw: Special Education Legal Developments and Cases 2015 is divided into four Chapters.

Chapter 1 introduces legal terms and concepts. You learn about statutes, regulations, case law, judicial interpretations, and factors that cause law to evolve and change. This chapter includes an overview of the federal laws that govern the education of children with disabilities.

Chapter 2 is about legal news and developments. This chapter includes developing law about "exhaustion of administrative remedies" in a case that may be decided by the Supreme Court. You will learn about jury trials and verdicts, monetary damages, and multi-million dollar settlements in teacher abuse cases.

Chapter 2 also includes actions and opinions from the U.S. Department of Justice (DOJ) and U. S. Department of Education in "Dear Colleague" letters from the Office of Special Education and Rehabilitation Services (OSERS) and the Office of Special Education Programs (OSEP).

Chapter 3 begins with a Table of Decisions by Courts of Appeals in 2015. This Table of Decisions includes the date, court, synopsis of the legal issues, outcome, and prevailing party in each case. Each case in the Table of Decisions is linked to a summary of the case. We used the Court's words to describe the issues in the case and the rulings. Each decision includes a link to the full text of the decision as published in Google Scholar.

Chapter 4 is about legal research. This chapter includes a tutorial about how to use Google Scholar as a legal research tool. Google Scholar is an accessible search engine that indexes the full text of federal and state legal decisions.

An Index is at the end of the book. In addition to the Table of Contents and index, the search feature in *Wrightslaw: Special Education Legal Developments and Cases 2015* is a fast, easy way to locate information on issues that are of interest to you.

Assume you want to locate information about "abuse." You can use the "Find" or "Search" commands to find all entries of "abuse" in the book. An easier strategy is to use the "Control" or "Command" shortcut keys (depending on whether you are using a Windows or Apple computer) and the letter "F."

Wrightslaw: Special Education Legal Developments and Cases 2015 is a legal reference book. We suggest that you begin by reviewing Chapters 1, 2, and the Table of Decisions in Chapter 3.

We recommend that you skim the case summaries that follow the Table of Decisions in Chapter 3. Next, read Chapter 4 and practice finding cases on Google Scholar.

After you finish the Google Scholar Tutorial, return to the case summaries in Chapter 3.

Links in the Table of Decisions in Chapter 3 will allow you to download the full text of decisions from Google Scholar.

In Summation

Now that you've finished reading this Introduction, you have a clearer sense of how this book is organized and how to get the most out of the book. In Chapter 2, you'll catch up on legal news and see how the law is evolving.

When you learn about this new information, you may feel excited too!

Chapter 1. Legal Concepts and Education Laws

This chapter introduces legal terms and concepts.

You will learn about the four types of law: federal and state constitutions, statutes, regulations, and case law. Case law refers to judicial interpretations of statutes and regulations that cause law to evolve and change.

An overview of the federal laws that govern the education of children with disabilities follows. These laws include the Individuals with Disabilities Act (IDEA), Section 504 of the Rehabilitation Act (Section 504), the Americans with Disabilities Act Amendment Act (ADA AA), the Every Student Succeeds Act (ESSA), the Family Educational and Rights and Privacy Act (FERPA), and the McKinney-Vento Homeless Assistance Act.

Constitutional Law

The United States Constitution outlines the structure of the federal government. All laws passed must agree with the principles and rights set forth in the Constitution.

The first ten amendments to the Constitution are called the Bill of Rights. The Bill of Rights is the source of the most fundamental rights – such as freedom of speech and religion,[1] protection against unreasonable searches and seizures,[2] and protection from cruel and unusual punishment.[3] Later, the Fourteenth Amendment was added and titled "Civil Rights" but is better known as the "Equal Protection Clause."[4] These Amendments[5] were added to the Constitution to protect citizens against interference from the federal government.

States must ensure that their statutes and regulations are consistent with the United States Code (U.S.C.) and the Code of Federal Regulations (CFR). While state laws and

---

[1] First Amendment

[2] Fourth Amendment

[3] Eighth Amendment

[4] Fourteenth Amendment - "nor shall any State deprive any person of life, liberty, or property, without due process of law; nor deny to any person within its jurisdiction the equal protection of the laws."

[5] http://www.ushistory.org/documents/amendments.htm

regulations may provide more rights than federal laws, they cannot provide fewer rights than guaranteed by federal law.

If a state law or regulation is in direct conflict with a federal law, federal law controls, pursuant to the "Supremacy Clause" of the U. S. Constitution.[6]

Statutes

Statutes are laws passed by federal, state, and local legislatures. The original federal special education law was the "Education for All Handicapped Children Act of 1975." This law has been reauthorized and renamed several times since 1975.

When Congress reauthorized the law in 2004, it was titled as the "Individuals with Disabilities Education Improvement Act"[7] but is commonly referred to as "IDEA 2004" to distinguish it from the earlier 1997 version, known as IDEA 97.

Regulations & Commentary

After Congress reauthorized the Individuals with Disabilities Education Act in 2004, the U.S. Department of Education (USDOE) developed proposed special education regulations. The USDOE published the proposed regulations in the *Federal Register* (F.R.) and solicited comments from citizens and stakeholders.

On August 14, 2006, the final IDEA 2004 Regulations and an Analysis of Comments and Changes (Commentary) were published in the *Federal Register*.[8]

The IDEA 2004 regulations[9] are published in Volume 34, Part 300 of the Code of Federal Regulations. The legal citation for the regulations is 34 CFR Part 300.

A regulation must be consistent with the law and may provide more details and specifics that the statute and is considered to have the "force of law."

State Law and Regulations

State constitutions establish the structure of state government. States must develop special education statutes and regulations that are consistent with the United States Code (U.S.C.) and the Code of Federal Regulations (CFR). State statutes and regulations may provide more rights than federal law but may not take away rights provided by federal law.

---

[6] U. S. Constitution, Article VI, Clause 2 – "This Constitution . . . shall be the supreme law of the land; and the judges in every state shall be bound thereby . . ."

[7] 20 U.S.C. §1400(a) - See Wrightslaw: Special Education Law, 2nd Ed., page 45

[8] http://www.wrightslaw.com/idea/commentary.htm

[9] For the IDEA regulations, see *Wrightslaw*, page 187.

Federal Education Statutes

Several federal statutes affect the education of children with disabilities, including:

- Individuals with Disabilities Education Act, known as IDEA, beginning at 20 U.S.C. §1400, *et seq.*

- Section 504 of the Rehabilitation Act beginning at 29 U.S.C. § 794 *et seq.*

- Americans with Disabilities Act Amendments Act of 2008, known as ADA AA, codified as 42 USCA § 12101, *et seq.*

- Every Student Succeeds Act of 2015, known as ESSA, is the successor to the No Child Left Behind Act of 2001 and is a reauthorization of the Elementary and Secondary Education Act of 1965 (ESEA) begins at 20 U.S.C. § 6301, *et seq.*

- Family Educational and Rights and Privacy Act, known as FERPA, begins at 20 U.S.C. § 1232, *et seq.*

- McKinney-Vento Homeless Assistance Act which begins at 42 U.S.C. § 11431, *et seq.*

Individuals with Disabilities Education Act (IDEA 2004)

The most important statute in IDEA is the "Purposes" of the law, located in Section 1400(d). The statement of Purposes is your mission statement. The main purposes of IDEA are:

> [To] ensure that all children with disabilities have available to them a free appropriate public education that emphasizes **special education and related services designed to meet their unique needs** and **prepare them for further education, employment and independent living** . . . [and] to ensure that the **rights of children** with disabilities **and parents** of such children **are protected** ...[10]

Section 1401 of IDEA includes thirty-six legal definitions in alphabetical order. Read these definitions carefully, especially the definitions of child with a disability, free appropriate public education, related services, special education, supplementary aids and services, and transition services.[11]

Child with a Disability[12]

If you are a parent, the most important definition is likely to be "child with a disability." Your child's classification as a "child with a disability" determines whether your child is eligible for special education and related services under the law.

---

[10] 20 U.S.C. §1400(d), see *Wrightslaw*, page 48.

[11] 20 U.S.C. §1401, see *Wrightslaw*, page 49.

[12] 20 U.S.C. §1401(3), see *Wrightslaw*, page 49.

A child with a disability is **not** automatically eligible for special education and related services under IDEA. To be eligible for a free appropriate public education under the IDEA, a child must meet two criteria. The child must have a disability and "by reason thereof, **needs special education and related services**" (emphasis added). Over time, courts have held that the child's disability must "adversely affect" educational performance.

If a child has a disability but does not need "special education and related services," the child will not be eligible under IDEA but may be eligible for accommodations and protections under Section 504 of the Rehabilitation Act.

Free Appropriate Public Education (FAPE)[13]

The term '**free appropriate public education**' means special education and related services that–

(A) have been provided at public expense, under public supervision and direction, and without charge;

(B) meet the standards of the State educational agency;

(C) include an appropriate preschool, elementary school, or secondary school education in the State involved; and

(D) are provided in conformity with the individualized education program required under Section 1414(d) of this title.

In *Board of Education v. Rowley,*[14] the U.S. Supreme Court clarified that children with disabilities are entitled to access to an education that provides educational benefit. They were not entitled to the "best" education, nor were they entitled to an education that would "maximize" their potential.[15]

After reviewing the legislative history of Education for All Handicapped Children Act (now IDEA), the Court in *Rowley* held:

> ... [T]he intent of the Act was more to open the door of public education to handicapped children on appropriate terms than to guarantee any particular level of education once inside ... We conclude that the "basic floor of opportunity" provided by the Act consists of access to specialized instruction and related services which are individually designed to provide educational benefit to the child.

Related Services[16]

Related services are services the child needs to benefit from special education and include:

---

[13] 20 U.S.C. §1401(9), see *Wrightslaw*, page 51.

[14] 458 U.S. 176 (1982), see *Wrightslaw*, page 343.

[15] The full text of the decision in *Rowley* is in *Wrightslaw*, page 343.

[16] 20 U.S.C. §1401(26), see *Wrightslaw*, page 54.

[T]ransportation, and such developmental, corrective, and other supportive services (including speech-language pathology and audiology services, interpreting services, psychological services, physical and occupational therapy, recreation) . . . designed to enable a child with a disability . . . to benefit from special education . . .

Special Education[17]

The law defines "special education" as "specially designed instruction . . . to meet the unique needs of a child with a disability . . ."

If the child has a disability and an IEP, the school must provide physical education as part of the child's special education program.[18] Many children benefit from adapted physical education (APE). Because physical education is a required component of special education, the child's physical education teacher should be included as a member of the IEP team.[19]

Supplementary Aids and Services[20]

The IDEA defines supplementary aids and services as:

> . . . [A]ids, services, and other supports that are provided in **regular education classes** . . . to enable children with disabilities to be educated with nondisabled children [in the least restrictive environment].

The school must provide nonacademic and extracurricular services and activities so children with disabilities have an equal opportunity to participate in school services and activities. Supplemental services include athletics, transportation, recreational activities, special interest groups or clubs sponsored by the school, employment assistance.[21]

Transition Services[22]

The goal of transition is to improve the child's academic and functional achievement and to facilitate the child's movement from school to employment and further education. Transition services must be based on "the individual child's needs, taking into account the child's strengths, preferences, and interests."

Commentary to the IDEA Regulations

When the Department of Education published the Regulations for IDEA 2004, they included an "Analysis of Comments and Changes,"[23] also known as the "Commentary."

---

[17] 20 U.S.C. §1401(29), see *Wrightslaw*, page 55.

[18] 20 U.S.C. §1401(29)(B), see *Wrightslaw*, page 55.

[19] For the legal requirements for Physical Education and Adapted Physical Education, see http://www.wrightslaw.com/info/pe.index.htm

[20] 20 U.S.C. §1401(33), see *Wrightslaw*, page 55.

[21] 34 C.F.R. §300.107 – Nonacademic services, see Wrightslaw, page 206.

[22] 20 U.S.C. §1401(34), see *Wrightslaw*, page 56.

[23] http://www.wrightslaw.com/idea/commentary.htm

The Commentary describes terms, definitions, and requirements in clear language.[24]

When you are wrestling with the meaning of a regulation, read the discussion about that regulation in the Commentary. The Commentary will help you understand the decision to write the regulation as it is. The Commentary will also help you understand different perspectives on a particular regulation.

Section 504 of the Rehabilitation Act of 1973

Section 504 of the Rehabilitation Act is a civil rights law that prohibits discrimination against individuals with disabilities. Title II prohibits discrimination on the basis of disability by state and local governments.

Section 504 is intended to ensure that children with disabilities have equal access to education. The Purposes of Section 504 are:

> To empower individuals with disabilities to maximize employment, economic self-sufficiency, independence, and inclusion and integration into society . . .
>
> . . .
>
> No otherwise qualified individual with a disability in the United States . . . shall, solely by reason of her or his disability, be excluded from the participation in, be denied the benefits of, or be subjected to discrimination under any program or activity receiving Federal financial assistance . . .[25]

There are significant differences between a FAPE under Section 504 and a FAPE under IDEA. A free appropriate public education (FAPE) under Section 504 requires the school to provide regular or special education aids and services that meet the child's educational needs as adequately as the needs of non-disabled students are met.[26]

A free appropriate public education (FAPE) under IDEA requires the school to provide an Individualized Education Program (IEP) that is designed to meet the child's unique needs and provide the child with educational benefit.[27]

Children and parents have fewer procedural protections under Section 504 than under the IDEA. IDEA includes an elaborate system of procedural safeguards designed to protect the child and parents. These safeguards include written notice before any change of placement and the right to an independent educational evaluation at public expense. Section 504 does not include these protections.

---

[24] Download the full text of the Regulations and Commentary or specific portions such as Evaluations, IEPs, etc., from http://www.wrightslaw.com/idea/commentary.htm

[25] 20 U.S.C. §794, see *Wrightslaw*, page 291.

[26] Section 504 regulations state that a "free appropriate public education [is] the provision of regular or special education and related aids and services that . . . are designed to meet individual educational needs of persons with disabilities as adequately as the needs of persons without disabilities are met." 34 C.F.R. § 104.33(b)(1)

[27] *Rowley*, 458 U.S. 176 (1982).

Americans with Disabilities Act Amendments Act (ADA AA)

Congress amended the Americans with Disabilities Act (ADA) in 2008. It is known as both "ADA" and "ADA AA" the latter "AA" referring to "Amendments Act." In 2008, the amendments to ADA broadened the definition of disability.[28] Section 504 incorporates the ADA by reference and it applies to all public school students. Americans with Disabilities Amendment Act (ADA AA)

Title II of the ADA states: "No qualified individual with a disability shall, by reason such disability, be excluded from participation in or be denied the benefits of the services, programs, or activities of a public entity, or be subjected to discrimination by any such entity."[29]

Wrightslaw Note: Section 504 is codified at 29 U.S.C. § 794. Implementing regulations are at 34 CFR. Part 104 and 34 CFR. Part 104 Appendix A. Title II of the ADA is codified at 42 U.S.C. § 12131- 12132. Implementing regulations are at 28 CFR. Part 35. Title III of the ADA about public accommodations such as private, non-religious schools is at 42 U.S.C. §§ 12182-12182(b)(1)(E). Implementing regulations are at 28 CFR Part 36.

Every Student Succeeds Act of 2015 (ESSA)

In December 2015, the No Child Left Behind Act of 2001 (NCLB) was replaced by the Every Student Succeeds Act (ESSA). NCLB and the ESSA are new versions of the original Elementary and Secondary Education Act of 1965 (ESEA) which begins at 20 U.S.C. § 6301, *et seq*.

The purpose of the ESSA is "to provide all children significant opportunity to receive a fair equitable, and high quality education, and to close educational achievement gaps."[30]

Wrightslaw Note: After the Statement of Purpose, you may be surprised when you read the list of actions that the Secretary of Education is forbidden from taking. Although Congress intended to reduce the federal role in education, Congress did not reduce federal education funding.

The Advocacy Institute has collected an impressive library of resources about ESSA.[31]

---

[28] 42 U.S.C. § 12102(4)(A) - "shall be construed in favor of broad coverage" . . . and includes disabilities that are "episodic" such as diabetes, epilepsy and allergies. (42 U.S.C. § 12102(4)(D))

[29] 42 U.S.C. §12132

[30] The full text of ESSA is located on our website at http://www.wrightslaw.com/essa/essa.391pages.pdf

[31] Every Student Succeeds Act Resources at http://www.advocacyinstitute.org/ESSA/index.shtml

Family Education Rights and Privacy Act (FERPA)

The Family Education Rights and Privacy Act (FERPA)[32] is a federal statute with the purpose of protecting the privacy of education records.

FERPA addresses issues about education records that include but are not limited to:

- Rights to inspect and review educational records

- Procedures to amend education records

- Conditions and consent for disclosure of personally identifiable information from education records

- Enforcement procedures[33]

FERPA applies to all agencies and institutions that receive federal funds, including elementary and high schools, colleges, and universities.

The FERPA statute is in the United States Code at 20 U.S.C. § 1232g and 1232h. The FERPA regulations are in the Code of Federal Regulations at 34 CFR Part 99. The FERPA regulations are written in an easy-to-read Frequently Asked Question format.[34] If you have a question about a FERPA issue, you are likely to find the answer in these regulations.

McKinney-Vento Homeless Assistance Act[35]

The McKinney-Vento Homeless Assistance Act requires all school districts to ensure that each child of a homeless parent and each homeless child shall have equal access to the same free, appropriate public education as provided to children and youth who are not homeless.

The McKinney-Vento Homeless Assistance Act includes several requirements including:

- School districts *shall* make decisions in the best interest of the child;

- School districts *must* immediately enroll homeless children, even if medical, academic and residency **records are not available;** and

- School districts *shall not* "segregate homeless children in separate schools or separate programs within a school, based on the child's status as homeless."[36]

---

[32] 20 U.S.C. §1232g, *et. seq.* See *Wrightslaw*, page 307.

[33] 34 CFR § 99.31.

[34] http://www.ecfr.gov/cgi-bin/text-idx?rgn=div5&node=34:1.1.1.1.33

[35] 42 U.S.C. §11431, *et. seq.*, see *Wrightslaw*, page 319.

[36] 42 U.S.C. §11432(e)(3).

Evolving Case Law & Judicial Interpretations

Case Law

As you read decisions in *Wrightslaw: Special Education Legal Developments and Cases 2015*, you will see inconsistencies from one court to another. You will also see how a particular issue, such as "Exhaustion," has evolved from decisions issued years ago.

Special education litigation usually begins with a due process hearing.[37]

Within the state due process structure, there are "single-tier"[38] states and "two-tier"[39] states. In a single-tier state, after the Hearing Officer or Administrative Law Judge issues a decision, the losing party can appeal to federal or state court. In a two-tier state, the losing party must first appeal to the state department of education to have a Review Officer or Review Panel appointed. After the Review Officer issues a decision, the losing party can then appeal to federal or state court.

State courts and federal courts are different judicial systems. As a rule, after a case is filed in state or federal court, it will remain in that system. Cases filed in state court usually remain in the state court system while cases filed in federal district courts generally remain in the federal court system. Occasionally, a state court case may be "removed" to federal court and a federal case may be remanded back to state court dependent upon whether there is a "Federal Question" contained within the pleadings or earlier decisions.

Most appeals of Due Process and Review decisions in special education cases are filed in federal court (U. S. District Court). The losing party at the District Court level can file an appeal in their U. S. Court of Appeals. Table 1 lists the states in each appeals court.

A Court of Appeals panel consists of three judges. After a decision is issued, the losing party may ask the U. S. Supreme Court to hear the case.

Before appealing to the Supreme Court, the losing party may petition the Court of Appeals for an *En Banc* hearing, i.e., a hearing before the full panel of the Court of Appeals judges. The basis to request an *En Banc* hearing is that the "panel decision conflicts with a decision of the U. S. Supreme Court or of [that circuit] court . . . and consideration by the full court is therefore necessary to secure and maintain uniformity of the court's decisions . . ."[40]

---

[37] 20 U.S.C. §1415(f) see *Wrightslaw*, page 112.

[38] 20 U.S.C. §1415(i) see *Wrightslaw*, page 115.

[39] 20 U.S.C. §1415(g) see *Wrightslaw*, page 116.

[40] FRAP 35(b)(1)(A).

Legal Interpretations

Law is subject to different interpretations. If you read an article about a special education decision, the interpretations and conclusions in that article will reflect the opinions and biases of the author. If you read the case on your own, your interpretations and conclusions of the case may be quite different. This is why it is so important for you to read cases, statutes, and regulations yourself, instead of relying on the opinions of others.

When a case has compelling facts, the judge(s) may write a decision that is contrary to the current case law in that Circuit. To support this decision, the judge may find and use unique facts within the case or a loophole in the law to create an "exception to the general rule." Decisions that are "exceptions to the general rule" cause the body of law to change and grow.

When you read an article about a changing area of law, the author may note that the "General Rule" or "Majority Rule" has been "swallowed up by the exceptions to the rule," so that the exceptions have now become the general rule.

When Congress wants to pass a law but is unable to agree on the wording of the law, members often compromise by using vague language in the bill. Vague words and phrases in statutes are confusing but are normal in all laws.

Confusing words and phrases lead to litigation. As you will see in ***Wrightslaw: Special Education Legal Developments and Cases 2015,*** the legal definition of an "appropriate education" and "educational benefit" is still being litigated today, decades after the U.S. Supreme Court issued their decision in *Rowley*.

When courts agree on an interpretation, a majority rule usually evolves. A minority rule may also develop. If a majority rule does not develop, the legal issue becomes more confusing with conflicting rulings from different courts on the same issue.

As happened in *Carter*, U. S. Courts of Appeal in different circuits issue conflicting rulings on an issue. Conflicting rulings lead to "splits between circuits." The U.S. Supreme Court often declines to accept a case for Certiorari unless there is a split between circuits that needs to be resolved.

U. S. Courts of Appeal - Twelve Circuits

As you see in Table 1, all states and territories are in one of the twelve circuits. Which Circuit is your state in?

Table 1: States In Each Circuit
1st Circuit: MA, ME, NH, RI, PR
2nd Circuit: CT, NY, VT
3rd Circuit: DE, NJ, PA, USVI
4th Circuit: MD, NC, SC, VA, WV
5th Circuit: LA, MS, TX
6th Circuit: KY, MI, OH TN
7th Circuit: IL, IN, WI
8th Circuit: AR, IA, MN, MO, ND, NE, SD
9th Circuit: AK, AZ, CA, HI, ID, MT, NV, OR, WA
10th Circuit: CO, KS, NM, OK, UT, WY
11th Circuit: AL, FL, GA
DC Circuit: Washington, DC

When a federal judge in your state issues a decision that provides a new definition or legal standard, that decision is not binding on federal judges in other states. If that judge's ruling is appealed, the appeal will be filed in your Circuit.

When the Court of Appeals issues a decision on that new definition or legal standard, that ruling is binding on all district courts in your Circuit but it is not binding on federal courts in other Circuits.

It is not unusual for one circuit to issue a ruling that is in direct conflict with another circuit. That is what happened in the author's *Carter* case when the Fourth Circuit issued their ruling.[41]

Previously, the Second Circuit had issued a decision in *Tucker*.[42] *Tucker* held that parents could not be reimbursed for private school tuition, even if the public school's IEP was not appropriate, if the private program was not on the state's approved list and the teachers were not certified or licensed by the state.

In *Carter*,[43] the Fourth Circuit held that reimbursement is proper if the private program is appropriate, even if the program is not on the state's approved list and the teachers are not certified by the state. The Supreme Court upheld the Fourth Circuit's decision.

Split Between Circuits / U. S. Supreme Court Appeal

When two or more circuits issue conflicting rulings on a legal issue, this is known as a "split between circuits." As a general rule, the Supreme Court will not hear a case unless there is a split between circuits or the case presents a significant issue of public policy.

A petition for a writ of certiorari is rarely granted when the asserted error consists of erroneous factual findings or the misapplication of a properly stated rule of law." See Rule 10 of the *Rules of the Supreme Court of the United States*.[44]

Decisions by the U. S. Supreme Court are the "law of the land" and are binding in all courts in the country.

Legal Research

When you are researching a legal issue, you need to study:

- United States Code, *i.e.*, the Statute

- Federal Regulations, the "*Commentary*," State Regulations and State Law

- Judicial decisions, also known as case law

---

[41] *Carter v. Florence County Sch. Dist. IV*, 950 F.2d 156 (4ᵗʰ Cir. 1991) is at http://www.wrightslaw.com/law/caselaw/case_carter_4cir.htm

[42] *Tucker v. Bay Shore Union Free School District*, 873 F.2d 563 (2d Cir. 1989).

[43] *Florence County Sch. Dist. IV v. Carter (4th Cir. 1991)*, 950 F.2d 156 (4th Cir. 1991).

[44] Rules of the Supreme Court of the United States (2013) are at http://www.supremecourt.gov/ctrules/2013RulesoftheCourt.pdf

When you have a question about a legal issue, read the United States Code section about your issue first. Check the footnotes at the bottom of **Wrightslaw: Special Education Law, 2nd Edition** to see if we discussed that statute.

Next, read the federal regulation about the issue. Then, read the Commentary to the Regulations to get a clearer sense of disputed issues in the regulation. You should expect to read the Code and regulation more than once.

After you have an understanding about the federal law and regulation, read your state statute and regulation. In many instances, you will find that the state law / regulation is a verbatim copy and paste of the federal law . . . but not always. Note any differences between federal and state law. Most states have very few special education statutes with the bulk of state law contained in the state regulations.

When you find cases about your issue, read the earlier decisions first before reading recent decisions. If you know a case was appealed, read the earlier decision that was appealed and reversed or affirmed. When you read early decisions first, you will have a clearer sense of how the law on this issue is evolving. You will be in a stronger position to predict the future course of that law.[45]

When one court takes a position that the law is clear, another court is likely to interpret the law differently and arrive at a different opinion. This is the nature of law.

Legal Citations - U.S.C. / F.3d

References to law are called legal citations. Legal citations are standardized formats that explain where you will find a particular statute, regulation, or case. When you see a legal citation such as 20 U.S.C. § 1400 *et seq.*, the term "*et seq.*" means beginning in Volume 20 in the United States Code at Section 1400 and continuing thereafter.

In the *United States Code*, the "Findings and Purposes" of the IDEA are in Section 1400 of Title 20. The legal citation for Findings and Purposes is 20 U.S.C. § 1400. You may refer to Findings and Purposes as "20 U.S.C. § 1400" or "Section 1400."

Legal decisions issued by the Courts of Appeal are published in the *Federal Reporter, Third Edition*. Decisions are cited as volume number, F.3d, followed by page number, with the Circuit and year in parentheses.

The third edition of the *Federal Reporter* for the Courts of Appeal has passed volume 800. After 999 F.3d is published, legal citations will change to the Fourth Edition.

---

[45] For example, a split is building between circuits about the term, "educational benefit." Does it mean "some educational benefit" or "meaningful educational benefit?" Some courts have held that Congress heightened the *Rowley* standard while other courts disagree.

Decisions in the first edition of the *Federal Reporter* published between 1825 and 1925 are cited as F.1d. Court of Appeals cases published between 1925 and 1993 were published in F.2d until 1993 when the first edition of F.3d was published.

Some cases in ***Wrightslaw: Special Education Legal Developments and Cases 2015*** will not be published in the *Federal Reporter, Third Edition*, so there will not be a "F.3d" legal citation for these cases. If the "F.3d" citation is available when this book is published, we will include the citation. When a Court of Appeals believes that a decision is not noteworthy or does not create new law, the case will not be published in the Federal Reporter, *i.e.,* F.3d.

Wrightslaw: Special Education Legal Developments and Cases 2015 contains most Court of Appeals cases issued in 2015.

The first case in the Table of Decisions is *Fort Bend Ind. Sch Dist v. Douglas A. Fort Bend* is cited as 779 F.3d 959 (5th Cir. 2015). This citation means the decision is published in Volume 779 of F.3d, beginning on page 959 and was issued by the Court of Appeals for the Fifth Circuit in 2015.

Do Not Publish / FRAP 32.1

As you read these cases, you may notice a statement at the beginning such as "Not Precedential," "Do Not Publish," or "Not for Publication." This does not mean that you cannot publish the decision or that you cannot rely on the decision as law.

Unless a decision includes other restrictions, "Do Not Publish" usually means that, in the opinion of the judges on that panel, the decision is not noteworthy, does not create new legal precedent, and should not be published in the *Federal Reporter, 3rd Edition* (F.3d).

The notation "Do Not Publish" is addressed in Rule 32.1, "Citing Judicial Dispositions" in the *Federal Rules of Appellate Procedure (FRAP)*.[46]

All cases in ***Wrightslaw: Special Education Legal Developments and Cases 2015*** are available from Google Scholar, a publicly accessible electronic database, and can be disseminated.

---

[46] "A court may not prohibit or restrict the citation of federal judicial opinions, orders, judgments, or other written dispositions that have been designated as 'unpublished,' 'not for publication,' 'non-precedential,' 'not precedent,' or the like; [and that] if a party cites a federal judicial opinion, order, judgment, or other written disposition that is not available in a publicly accessible electronic database, the party must file and serve a copy of that opinion, order, judgment, or disposition with the brief or other paper in which it is cited." (FRAP 32.1)

In Summation

In this chapter, you learned about statutes, regulations, case law, judicial interpretations, and how law evolves. You also learned about legal research and legal citations.

In the next chapter, you will dive into legal news, developments, and cases.

This page intentionally left blank.

Chapter 2. Special Education Legal News & Developments

In this chapter, you will learn about news and developing areas of special education law. One developing area is the requirement that parents request a special education due process hearing before filing a lawsuit in court.

Service dog cases are another growing area of law. Service dog cases are usually brought under the Americans with Disabilities Act (ADA), not the Individuals with Disabilities Education Act (IDEA). A Court of Appeals decision in a service dog case for damages is on appeal to the U.S. Supreme Court.

Another developing area is the apparent increase in the number of cases resulting in large verdicts and settlements for children with disabilities. You will learn about jury trials in teacher abuse cases that led to multi-million dollar verdicts and settlements. Several teacher abuse cases are pending and will be discussed later in this chapter.

This chapter also includes Memoranda and Dear Colleague Policy Letters issued by the Office of Special Education and Rehabilitative Services (OSERS) and the Office of Special Education Programs (OSEP) in 2015.

Legal News and Developments

Exhaustion of Administrative Remedies

The "Rule of Construction" statute at 20 U.S.C. § 1415(l) states:

> Nothing in this title shall be construed to restrict or limit the rights, procedures, and remedies available under the Constitution, the Americans with Disabilities Act of 1990, [42 U.S.C. §12101] title V of the Rehabilitation Act of 1973, [29 U.S.C. § 790] or other Federal laws protecting the rights of children with disabilities, except that before the filing of a civil action under such laws seeking relief that is also available

under this part, the procedures under subsections (f) and (g) shall be exhausted to the same extent as would be required had the action been brought under this part.[47]

The requirement that due process procedures in subsections (f) and (f)[48] "shall be exhausted" is known as "exhaustion of administrative remedies." If a parent believes that their child's IEP is not appropriate, the parent cannot initially file a lawsuit to contest the IEP in Federal or State Court. The parent must first request a special education due process hearing. After the due process hearing (and in some states, a review hearing) is completed, the losing party can file a lawsuit in Federal Court.

The law on this issue is evolving. Some Courts have held that if exhaustion is considered "futile," the parent does not need to exhaust. For example, if the parent is seeking relief that is not available under the IDEA - such as monetary damages - exhaustion is not required. Other courts have held the parent must exhaust, even if the child does not have an IEP and the sole issue is recovery of dollar damages.

A case about whether "exhaustion" is required – *Fry v. Napoleon* - is pending at the Supreme Court but SCOTUS has not yet granted "Cert."

Cases Dismissed for Failure to Exhaust Administrative Remedies

In 2015, cases brought under Section 504 /ADA were dismissed in the 3rd, 6th, 9th, 10th, and 11th Circuits because parents did not exhaust their administrative remedies (request due process hearings) under the Individuals with Disabilities Education Act. These cases are listed in chronological order.

A Petition for Certiorari is pending before the U. S. Supreme Court in the *Fry* case. The last case listed, *MS v. Marple*, was dismissed for failure to exhaust although the child never had an IEP. More about these cases in Chapter 3.

Cases dismissed for failure to exhaust in 2015 include:

> *Lainey C. v. Hawaii Dept. of Ed.* (9th Circuit)
>
> *Laura A. v. Limestone Bd. Ed.* (11th Circuit)
>
> *Fry v. Napoleon Comm Sch Dist.* (6th Circuit)
>
> *AF + Christine B. v. Espanola Pub. Sch.* (10th Circuit)
>
> *Carroll v. Lawton Indep Sch Dist.* (10th Circuit)
>
> *MS v. Marple Newtown School Dist.* (3rd Circuit)

---

[47] See *Wrightslaw: Special Education Law, 2nd Ed.*, page 123.

[48] 20 U.S.C.§ 1415(f) + (g), *Wrightslaw*, pages 112-116

Lainey C. v. Hawaii Dept. of Ed. (9th Circuit, 3/2/2015)

In *Lainey*, the parents of a child with autism requested a one-to-one aide to help their son with socialization. The Court accepted a behavioral specialist's opinion that providing an aide might cause the boy to be less independent and more socially isolated.

On appeal, the parents raised five new arguments about the inadequacy of the child's IEP that had not been raised at the due process hearing.

The Ninth Circuit held:

> This court has held that an argument not raised in an administrative complaint or due process hearing is not exhausted and cannot be raised for the first time on appeal to the district court.

Laura A. v. Limestone Bd. Ed. (11th Circuit, 4/28/2015)

In *Laura A*, the grandmother and "next friend" of J.O. requested a due process hearing to contest a finding that J.O. was no longer eligible for special education. In her letter requesting a due process hearing, she did not allege violations of Section 504. On appeal to district court, she alleged Section 504 violations.

The 11th Circuit upheld the district court's ruling that she failed to exhaust administrative remedies for her claim under Section 504.

Fry v. Napoleon Comm. Sch. Dist. (6th Circuit, 6/12/2015)

In *Fry v. Napoleon Comm. Sch. Dist.* a young child with multiple disabilities, including cerebral palsy, was prescribed a service dog to help with everyday tasks at home and at school. Her school refused to allow the service dog to accompany her in school.

After years of failed negotiations and disruptions in her education, her parents withdrew her from that school and enrolled her in a different school district. Her parents sued the school district for damages, alleging violations of Section 504 of the Rehabilitation Act and Title II of the Americans with Disabilities Act (ADA), and state disability law.

The child's parents did not request a special education due process hearing under IDEA, arguing that the exhaustion provision did not apply because they were not seeking relief available under IDEA. The school district filed a motion to dismiss, asserting that the parents' failure to exhaust their administrative remedies under IDEA required dismissal. The district court granted the school's motion to dismiss.

A divided court of appeals upheld the motion to dismiss and wrote an extensive description of the requirement to exhaust administrative remedies and the need for an "administrative record" created by a special education due process hearing:

> We have held that exhaustion is not required when the injuries alleged by the plaintiffs do not 'relate to the provision of a FAPE [free appropriate public education]' as defined by the IDEA, and when they cannot 'be remedied through the administrative process' created by that statute. When they do relate to the provision

of the child's education and can be remedied through IDEA procedures, waiving the exhaustion requirement would prevent state and local educational agencies from addressing problems they specialize in addressing and require courts to evaluate claims about educational harms that may be difficult for them to analyze without the benefit of an administrative record.

One judge on the panel wrote a strong dissent:

> The disability discrimination at issue is a text-book example of the harms that Section 504 and the ADA were designed to prevent, and the claims should not have been dismissed essentially because the victim of the discrimination was a school-aged child.
>
> ... even if the accommodation sought could be considered 'educational,' the fact that school policy would permit a 'guide dog' on campus, but not a certified 'service dog,' suggests why an attempt at exhaustion of administrative remedies would be futile in this case and should be excused.

In December 2015, the parents appealed this decision to the U.S. Supreme Court. In January 2016, the Court requested that the Solicitor General write a brief about whether the Court should hear this case.

We are tracking the *Fry* case. The SCOTUS pleadings, including the Petition for Cert, are available on Wrightslaw.com.[49]

AF + Christine B. v. Espanola Pub. Sch. (10th Circuit, 9/15/2015)

After requesting a due process hearing, the parent settled their IDEA claims at mediation and entered into a settlement agreement on their IDEA claims with the school. The parent then filed suit in federal court for damages pursuant to ADA and Section 504.

The District Court dismissed the suit because the parent failed to exhaust administrative remedies for their ADA and 504 claims. The Court of Appeals, in a split decision, upheld the District Court's decision.

> After ending her suit, she sought to begin it again. Despite the satisfactory result she received through mediation, Christine B ... thought she might sue — and she did.
>
> . . .
>
> Her lawsuit didn't seek to press a claim under IDEA, itself a tacit acknowledgment that her mediated settlement precluded that option. Instead, she sued under the Americans with Disabilities Act, the Rehabilitation Act, and 42 U.S.C. § 1983, though the allegations in her federal court complaint and those in her original IDEA administrative complaint are nearly identical: both allege that A.F. suffers from the same disabilities and both contend that the school district failed to take her disabilities into account in her educational program.

---

[49] http://www.wrightslaw.com/law/art/fry.napoleon.504.service.dog.htm

Carroll v. Lawton Indep. Sch Dist. (10th Circuit, 11/10/2015)

In this Oklahoma case, a special education teacher abused a child with autism. The child's parents filed a suit for damages under ADA and Section 504.

The District Court dismissed the parents' case because they did not first request a special education due process hearing, i.e., they failed to exhaust their administrative remedies. The 10th Circuit agreed:

> The single issue on appeal is whether the district court erred in determining the Carrolls' federal claims were subject to the IDEA's exhaustion requirement. We conclude the Carrolls' complaint alleges educational injuries that could be redressed to some degree by the IDEA's administrative remedies, we agree with the district court that exhaustion of those remedies was required.

MS. v. Marple Newtown Sch Dist. (3rd Circuit, 12/22/2015)

In *MS v. Marple*, the child had a 504 Plan, did not have an IEP, and did not receive special education services.

The Complaint asserted two claims under Section 504 and the ADA: (1) an accommodation claim based on the School District's failure to separate M.S. from her harassers, and (2) a retaliation claim based on the School District's response to complaints from M.S.'s mother.

The parent did not request a due process hearing before bringing suit.

Citing *Batchelor*, another decision from the Third Circuit, the appeals court held that the parent was required to request a due process hearing because the dispute was related to the child's "educational placement" or to "the provision of a free appropriate public education."

It is unknown whether the child was ever evaluated to determine eligibility for an IEP. It appears that she was not. As a part of the IDEA 2004 evaluation process, the parents are to be notified of the procedural safeguards and rights. If the parents were never provided with those rights, can a Court dismiss their case because they failed to exhaust administrative remedies pursuant to such an unknown right or responsibility?

Jury Trials, Monetary Damages, Settlements

Colorado Jury Awards $2.2 Million to Restrained Child in Ebonie S. v. Pueblo School District

On March 24, 2015, after a seven-day trial, a Colorado jury awarded $2.2 million in damages to a child with disabilities who was restrained in Kindergarten.

The Complaint alleged that the wrap-around table used to restrain Ebonie was only used with children with disabilities and that its use violated the Constitution, Section 504 of the Rehabilitation Act and the Americans with Disabilities Act (ADA).

The school district has appealed to the Court of Appeals for the Tenth Circuit.

> Complaint in *Ebonie S. v. Pueblo School District* [50]
>
> Jury Instructions in *Ebonie S. v. Pueblo School District* [51]
>
> Jury Verdict in *Ebonie S. v. Pueblo School District* [52]

Oregon Jury Awards $800,000 to Injured Child in Foster Smith v. Reynolds School District

On September 4, 2015, an Oregon jury awarded Foster Smith $800,000 after he sustained a devastating injury at school. Foster was born with Duchenne Muscular Dystrophy (DMD), a genetic disorder characterized by progressive muscle degeneration and weakness.[53] He needed an aide next to him whenever he walked.

Foster's team developed an IEP that provided for him to have a full-time aide or educational assistant next to him whenever he walked. Unknown to Foster's parents, the school reduced the number of aides in his school. Instead the full-time aide provided in his IEP, Foster had an aide who accompanied him for about 30 minutes a day, not "whenever he walked."

On the day of the accident, Foster's teacher and educational assistant watched as he walked 25-40 feet across the room alone, before falling to the floor. The educational assistant was not next to him. The Complaint alleged that because the school failed to provide Foster with an aide, as agreed to in his IEP, Foster fell, broke his leg, and will never be able to walk again.

During the trial, his mother testified that she tried to learn what happened to her son at school but the school refused to meet with her and froze her out. Foster went through six to eight weeks of physical therapy, but was not able to recover to the point where he could walk 10-15 feet. At the time of the trial, Foster was 13.

Foster Smith v. Reynolds was not brought as a violation of IDEA, Section 504, or the ADA. The case was brought as a simple personal injury negligence action.

On September 4, 2015, the jury awarded $800,000.

Jury awards $800k to boy who will never walk again after classroom fall by Aimee Green was published in the Oregonian/Oregon Live (September 4, 2015)[54]

Complaint for Personal Injury: Margo Smith as Guardian Ad Litem for Foster Smith, a minor, v. Reynolds School District.[55]

---

[50] http://www.wrightslaw.com/law/pleadings/CO.ebonie.amended.complaint.constitutionalviolation.pdf

[51] http://www.wrightslaw.com/law/pleadings/CO.ebonie.Jury.instruc.pdf

[52] http://www.wrightslaw.com/law/pleadings/CO.ebonie.Jury.verdict.2.2m.pdf

[53] https://www.mda.org/disease/duchenne-muscular-dystrophy

[54] http://www.oregonlive.com/portland/index.ssf/2015/09/jury_awards_boy_who_wont_ever.html

[55] http://www.wrightslaw.com/law/pleadings/OR.complaint.smith.jury.verdict.pdf

Ongoing Pattern of Physical Abuse: Garza v. Lansing Sch. Dist., et. al

On November 2, 2015, a Complaint[56] and later, an amended Complaint, [57] was filed in the Lansing, Michigan U. S. District Court on behalf of *Garza*. The Complaint alleged that special education teacher Duvall, an employee of Lansing School District, "has subjected the students in his classroom to severe physical, verbal and emotional / psychological abuse. Students were routinely subjected to Duvall's numerous unsanctioned, ineffective, unlawful and cruel methods."

The Complaint further alleged:

Duvall has a history of abusing students at LSD. For over a decade, staff, mental health professionals and parents notified LSD administrators and school officials about Duvall physically, verbally and psychologically abusing his students.

[The] LSD administrators received reports from parents, classroom aides and assistants that documented multiple instances of abuse that occurred on a daily basis at the hands of Duvall. . .

Not only did the supervisory personnel at Gardner and LSD conceal the abuse, they actively misrepresented Duvall's teaching abilities, even stating in his evaluations that he was an "excellent teacher."

We are following this case and will have updates on the Federal Court Complaints and Pleadings page[58] on Wrightslaw.com. Garza is represented by California attorney Peter Alfert.

Multi-Million Dollar Settlements in California Teacher Abuse Cases

Peter Alfert also represented the families of eight special education kindergarten students in a special education teacher abuse case. In California, the Antioch Unified school board voted to pay the families $8 million to settle a federal lawsuit over the abuse.

Mr. Alfert also represented families in a teacher abuse case against Rocklin Unified School District. In April 2015, two weeks after the District Attorney's Office filed criminal charges against a special education teacher, six families filed a federal lawsuit against the Rocklin Unified School District. As of October 2015, settlements totaling $5.3 million had been reached with five of the six families.[59]

---

[56] Original Complaint -
http://www.wrightslaw.com/law/pleadings/mi.complaint.abuse.2016.garza.v.lansing.pdf

[57] Amended Complaint -
http://www.wrightslaw.com/law/pleadings/mi.complaint.amended.abuse.2016.garza.v.lansing.pdf

[58] http://www.wrightslaw.com/law/pleadings/fed.court.complaints.htm

[59] "Three more families settle with Rocklin school district over suspected abuse by special education teacher" by Cathy Locke and Denny Walsh, published in the Sacramento Bee at http://www.sacbee.com/news/local/education/article41245200.html

The abuse of children with disabilities by school personnel is an expanding area of special education law. See "Pattern of Abuse of Special Needs Children Led Two Contra Costa School Districts to Pay Nearly $17 Million to Families in One Year."[60]

Discrimination under ADA and Section 504: Service Dog Cases

Family Appeals Ruling in Service Dog Case to Supreme Court: Fry v. Napoleon

On June 12, 2015, in *Fry v. Napoleon*, the Court of Appeals for the Sixth Circuit held that the child's parents were required to request a special education due process hearing, i.e., exhaust their administrative remedies, before they could file suit in federal court for damages under the ADA and Section 504.

In *Fry*, the child needed her service dog to accompany her at school but the school refused to allow the dog. When repeated attempts to resolve the dispute failed, the family enrolled their child in a school in a different jurisdiction and sued for dollar damages. Read the story of *Fry v. Napoleon*.

This ruling brought to light the inconsistent decisions from the Courts of Appeal about when parents must exhaust their administrative remedies. In October 2015, the parents filed a Petition for Certiorari (an appeal) with the U.S. Supreme Court.

In January 2016, the Supreme Court asked the Solicitor General to write a brief about whether they should hear this case.

> Complaint filed in U.S. District Court, Eastern District of Michigan[61]
>
> Decision from U.S. District Court, Eastern District of Michigan[62]
>
> Decision from U.S Court of Appeals for the Sixth Circuit[63]
>
> Petition for Writ of Certiorari[64]
>
> Brief in Opposition[65]

We will continue to follow this case and post updates on the *Fry v. Napoleon* page[66] at Wrightslaw.

---

[60] http://www.prnewswire.com/news-releases/attorneys-peter-alfert-and-todd-boley-announce-shocking-abuse-of-special-needs-preschoolers-leads-to-new-8-million-settlement-by-brentwood-union-school-district-241735031.html

[61] http://www.wrightslaw.com/law/pleadings/fry.complaint.distct.2012.pdf

[62] http://www.wrightslaw.com/law/caselaw/2014/mi.fry.napoleon.dist.ct.0110.pdf

[63] http://www.wrightslaw.com/law/caselaw/2015/6th.fry.napoleon.pdf

[64] http://www.wrightslaw.com/law/pleadings/fry.petition.cert.2015.10.pdf

[65] http://www.wrightslaw.com/law/pleadings/fry.brief.oppose.2015.12.pdf

[66] http://www.wrightslaw.com/law/art/fry.napoleon.504.service.dog.htm

Feds Sue New York District for Discrimination & Violation of Service Animal Requirements of ADA: DOJ v. Gates-Chili School District

On September 29, 2015, three months after the Sixth Circuit issued their decision in *Fry v. Napoleon*, the Department of Justice (DOJ) filed suit against the Gates-Chili Central School District. Why?

The Department of Justice claims that the school district discriminated against an eight-year-old child with disabilities and violated the service animal requirements of the ADA.

Background

Devyn is a third grader who has a neurodevelopmental genetic disorder called Angelman Syndrome, severe epilepsy, autism and other disabilities. Devyn is in a class for medically fragile children. She has an aide who helps with schoolwork and a nurse who administers medicine. She has limited communication via sign language and a speech-generating device.

Devyn also has a service dog named Hannah. Hannah is trained to spot the signals of a impending seizure and alert her caregivers. Hannah also keeps Devyn from wandering and provides mobility support so Devyn can walk independently.

When Devyn entered Kindergarten in 2012, the school district changed their policies and procedures to prohibit Devyn from bringing her service dog to school unless her parent provided a separate adult handler. The child's 1:1 aide or other school staff who help Devyn during the school day were not allowed to help.

In 2012, Devyn's mom filed a discrimination complaint with the Department of Justice.

Department of Justice Letter of Findings: April 13, 2015

On April 13, 2015, the Department of Justice issued a Letter of Findings of Fact and Conclusions of Law[67] under title II of the ADA. The Letter of Findings outlined the steps the District must take to meet its legal obligations and remedy violations of the ADA. DOJ ordered the school district to revise its policies and pay the family compensatory damages for injuries they suffered because the district failed to comply with the ADA.

The Gates-Chili Central School District refused to comply.

School District's Legal Fees

A local reporter filed a Freedom on Information request for the district's legal bills and obtained 38 pages of bills for 154 hours of legal work on the case in less than two years.

---

[67] http://www.ada.gov/briefs/gates-chili_lof.pdf

Special Education Legal Developments & Cases 2015

Between October 2013 and May 2015, the dispute about the service dog cost taxpayers more than $34,000 in legal fees - on top of the $17,000 a year that Devyn's mother had to pay for a handler who works about 15 minutes a day.[68]

Department of Justice Files Lawsuit: September 29, 2015

The lawsuit, filed in U.S. District Court in Rochester New York, alleges that the Gates-Chili School District violated Title II of the Americans with Disabilities Act (ADA). Read Complaint.[69]

"It is no longer acceptable – if ever it was – for a district to refuse reasonable modifications to a child who seeks to handle her own service dog . . . Certainly since passage of the American with Disabilities Act in 1990, such failure not only violates the dictates of conscience, it also violates the law" said U.S. Attorney William J. Hochul Jr. of the Western District of New York.[70]

---

[68] http://www.democratandchronicle.com/story/news/local/blogs/watchdog/2015/08/15/gates-chili-legal-fees-dog-devyn/31711985/

[69] http://www.ada.gov/gateschili/gateschili_complaint.html

[70] DOJ Press Release: https://www.justice.gov/opa/pr/justice-department-sues-gates-chili-central-school-district-violating-service-animal

Memos, Dear Colleague Letters and Policy Letters from OSERs and OSEP

January 2015

Due Process Hearings in Minnesota - Letter to Margaret O'Sullivan Kane (OSEP Policy Letter, 01/07/15) [71]

An individual wrote to the Secretary of Education with complaints about how due process hearings are conducted in Minnesota. The letter was forwarded to the Office of Special Education Programs (OSEP), Office of Special Education and Rehabilitative Services (OSERS), within the DOE. The complaints were about how school districts conduct hearings and time-limit restrictions on hearings. OSEP responded to similar complaints in 2010 and 2012 and quoted from one of their earlier letters:

> "Minnesota state law requires that the due process hearings conducted by the state be held in the local educational agency (LEA) responsible for the provision of FAPE at the time the hearing is conducted . . . [the] Court of Appeals for the Eighth Circuit has concluded that, due to this State statute, if "a student changes school districts and does not request a due process hearing, his or her right to challenge prior educational services is not preserved.

> "[T]hat the Minnesota statute, as interpreted by the Eighth Circuit to deny parents the right to file a due process complaint against an LEA that their child previously attended, provided that the violation occurred within two years of the date when the parents file the complaint - limits the parents' rights under the IDEA and is inconsistent with the provisions of 34 CFR §§300.507-300.518.

> "OSEP also believes that the section of the State Department of Education's Notice of Procedural Safeguards is . . . not consistent with the IDEA. However, decisions by the Eighth Circuit Court of Appeals are controlling on this point in the State of Minnesota."

The complainant cited decisions from other courts that rejected the Eighth Circuit's reasoning in *Thompson*. OSEP pointed out that decisions from appeals courts and district courts outside the Eighth Circuit are not binding on Minnesota.

On the time limit issue, the complainant reported that the MN Office of Administrative Hearings recommends that "[i]n all but exceptional circumstances, evidentiary hearings should be concluded within three hearing days of six hours each." OSEP responded:

> "The IDEA is silent on procedures related to the timing for presentation of evidence and regarding confrontation, cross-examination, and compelling the attendance of witnesses in a due process hearing. Hearing officers are authorized to determine procedural matters. States have some flexibility in establishing rules for conducting due process hearings.

---

[71] http://www2.ed.gov/policy/speced/guid/idea/memosdcltrs/acc-13-017562r-mn-kane-dph.pdf

"The guideline appears consistent with the requirements of IDEA - permits a hearing officer to extend the 18-hour time limitation for evidentiary hearings under exceptional circumstances. If a party believes that their rights have been violated, they have a right to appeal the decision to court."

Joint Guidance on English Language Learners (ELLs): Schools Must Act to Overcome Language Barriers (OSERS 01/07/15) [72]

On January 7, 2015, the Departments of Education (ED) and Justice (DOJ) released joint guidance reminding states, school districts and schools of their obligations under federal law to ensure that English learner students have equal access to a high-quality education and the opportunity to achieve their full academic potential. This guidance provides an outline of the legal obligations of State Education Agencies (SEA) and school districts to EL students under the civil rights laws.

Their "Dear Colleague" letter opens with:

"Forty years ago, the Supreme Court of the United States determined that in order for public schools to comply with their legal obligations under Title VI of the Civil Rights Act of 1964 (Title VI), they must take affirmative steps to ensure that students with limited English proficiency (LEP) can meaningfully participate in their educational programs and services."

The Joint Guidance Memorandum explained:

"That same year, Congress enacted the Equal Educational Opportunities Act (EEOA), which confirmed that public schools and State educational agencies (SEAs) must act to overcome language barriers that impede equal participation by students in their instructional programs.

"Ensuring that SEAs and school districts are equipped with the tools and resources to meet their responsibilities to LEP students, who are now more commonly referred to as English Learner (EL) students or English Language Learner students, is as important today as it was then.

"SEAs have a responsibility under the civil rights laws to provide appropriate guidance, monitoring, and oversight to school districts to ensure that EL students receive appropriate EL services. EL students are enrolled in nearly three out of every four public schools and their numbers are increasing. It is crucial to the future of our nation that these students have equal access to a high-quality education and the opportunity to achieve their full academic potential . . .

"In determining whether a school district's programs for EL students comply with the civil rights laws, the Department applies standards established by the United

---

[72] http://www2.ed.gov/about/offices/list/ocr/letters/colleague-el-201501.pdf

States Court of Appeals for the Fifth Circuit more than 30 years ago in *Castañeda v. Pickard*, 648 F.2d 989 (5th Cir. 1981)."

February 2015

Independent Educational Evaluations - Letter to Debbie Baus (OSEP Policy Letter, 02/23/15)[73]

Can a parent request an Independent Educational Evaluation (IEE) in an area that was not previously assessed by the school district's evaluation?

"When a parent disagrees with a school's evaluation because the school did not assess the child in a particular area, the parent has the right to request an IEE to assess the child in that area.

"If a parent requests an IEE at public expense, the school must (1) initiate a hearing to show that its evaluation is appropriate or (2) ensure that an IEE is provided at public expense."[74]

April 2015

Schools that Request a Due Process Hearing After Parent Files a State Complaint (OSEP Dear Colleague Letter, 04/15/15)[75]

Some school districts "may be filing due process complaints concerning the same issue that is the subject of an ongoing State complaint resolution, ostensibly to delay the State complaint process and force parents to participate in, or ignore at considerable risk, due process complaints and hearings ..." Schools that force parents who exercised "their right to file a State complaint into a more adversarial due process hearing harm the 'cooperative process' that should be the goal of all stakeholders."

Children with Disabilities with High Cognition - Letter to Delisle: 2e students (OSEP Letter to State Directors of Special Education, 4/17/2015)[76]

> *"I am writing to draw your attention to Letter to Delisle that addresses children with high cognition who may be eligible for special education and related services as a student with a specific learning disability . . .*

> *"In determining if a child has a disability, IDEA requires schools to use a variety of assessment tools and strategies . . . and prohibits the use of any single measure as the sole criterion . . . for determining whether a child is a child with a disability . . .*

> *"We continue to receive letters from people who work with children with disabilities with high cognition, expressing concerns that schools refuse to evaluate children with high cognition. I request that you distribute Letter to Delisle to your school districts*

---

[73] http://www2.ed.gov/policy/speced/guid/idea/memosdcltrs/acc-14-012562r-baus-iee.pdf

[74] 34 CFR §300.502(b)(2) See *Wrightslaw: Special Education Law, 2nd Ed.* page 252

[75] http://www2.ed.gov/policy/speced/guid/idea/memosdcltrs/dcl04152015disputeresolution2q2015.pdf

[76] http://www2.ed.gov/policy/speced/guid/idea/memosdcltrs/041715gilmantwiceevceptional2q2015.pdf

and remind them of the obligation to evaluate all children, regardless of cognitive skills . . ."

May 2015

State Identification and Correction of Noncompliance in Letter to Heather S. Deaton, Special Assistant Attorney General, Mississippi DOE - (OSEP Policy Letter, 05/19/15)[77]

Must the SEA require a school district to submit an improvement plan or must the SEA set aside its findings of noncompliance pending the outcome of a due process hearing?

What types of corrective actions may the SEA order to remedy a finding that a school district failed to provide a FAPE?

OSEP responded:

"An SEA must ensure that its school districts (LEAs) are in compliance with State and Federal requirements for educating children with disabilities. The SEA may not allow a district to delay implementing corrective actions pending the outcome of a due process hearing. The SEA must ensure corrective actions are completed as soon as possible and no more than one year from the date the State identified the noncompliance.

"The SEA is responsible for ensuring that child-specific or systemic noncompliance is corrected. When the SEA finds that a district failed to provide appropriate services, the SEA has broad flexibility to determine a remedy or corrective action. The remedy may include monetary reimbursement and compensatory services."

July 2015

Parentally Placed Private School Children with Disabilities Whose Parents Reside Outside the Country - Letter to Edward Sarzynski (OSEP Policy Letter, 07/06/15)[78]

The letter discusses "child find" when the child with a disability attends a private school located within a school district and the child's parents reside outside the country. It also discusses "Child Find" responsibilities for out-of-state students, i.e., when the child with a disability attends a private school in a state other than where the parents live.

Children with Autism Not Getting Needed Speech and Language Services (OSEP Dear Colleague Letter, 07/06/15)[79]

In a letter to school leaders, OSEP describes "concerns in the field about services delivered to children with autism spectrum disorders" including:

---

[77] http://www2.ed.gov/policy/speced/guid/idea/memosdcltrs/deaton051915findingsofnoncompliance2q2015.pdf

[78] http://www2.ed.gov/policy/speced/guid/idea/memosdcltrs/sarzynski070615parentallyplacedprivateschool3q2015.pdf

[79] http://www2.ed.gov/policy/speced/guid/idea/memosdcltrs/dclspeechlanguageautism0706153q2015.pdf

"Increasing numbers of children with autism spectrum disorders (ASD) are not receiving needed speech and language services from speech language pathologists at school.

"Speech-language pathologists are being left out of the evaluation process and eligibility determinations.

"Speech-language pathologists are not included or consulted in determining needs and the services provided in IEPs."

OSEP noted that:

"Some IDEA programs may be including applied behavior analysis (ABA) therapists exclusively without including, or considering input from, speech language pathologists and other professionals who provide different types of specific therapies that may be appropriate for children with ASD when identifying IDEA services for children with ASD."

Local Educational Agency (LEA) Maintenance of Effort (MOE) Questions and Answers (OSEP Dear Colleague Letter, July 27, 2015)[80]

In this letter, OSEP explains that:

"Generally, an LEA may not reduce the amount of local, or State and local, funds that it spends for the education of children with disabilities below the amount it spent for the preceding fiscal year."

September 2015

Joint Policy Statement on Inclusion of Children with Disabilities in Early Childhood Programs (09/14/15)[81]

All young children with disabilities need to have access to inclusive high-quality early childhood programs where they receive individualized, appropriate support.

The purpose of this policy statement is to recommend that States, school districts, schools, and private programs increase the inclusion of infants, toddlers, and preschool children with disabilities in high-quality early childhood programs.[82]

Due Process Hearings: Resolution Meetings, IEPs – In Letter to Matthew D. Cohen (OSEP Policy Letter, 09/16/15) [83]

Can a school district unilaterally amend a child's IEP during a resolution meeting and make the revised IEP the subject of the due process hearing?

---

[80] http://www2.ed.gov/policy/speced/guid/idea/memosdcltrs/osepmemo1510leamoeqa.pdf

[81] http://www2.ed.gov/policy/speced/guid/earlylearning/joint-statement-full-text.pdf

[82] Early childhood programs refer to those that provide early care and education to children birth through age five where the majority of children in the program are typically developing.

[83] http://www2.ed.gov/policy/speced/guid/idea/memosdcltrs/15-004400r-il-cohen-dph-9-9-15.pdf

Can an LEA submit an IEP that was drafted after the parent requested a hearing as its offer of a free appropriate public education (FAPE)?

OSEP responded that:

[T]he purpose of a resolution meeting is to achieve early resolution of the parent's complaint and to avoid the need for a costly, adversarial due process hearing and potential civil litigation . . . States have latitude in determining procedural rules for due process hearings so long as they are not inconsistent with the IDEA.

Is a Written Decision Required When SEA Accepts LEAs Proposal to Resolve State Complaint? Letter to Marcie Lipsitt (OSEP Policy Letter, 09/18/15)[84]

Is an SEA required to issue a written decision when the SEA accepts a school district's (LEA's) proposal to resolve a state complaint?

OSEP responded:

Once an SEA resolves a complaint . . . the SEA is required to issue a written decision to the complainant that addresses each allegation in the complaint and contains (1) findings of fact and conclusions; and (2) the reasons for the SEA's final decision.

October 2015

Policy guidance to clarify that the IDEA does not prohibit the terms dyslexia, dyscalculia, and dysgraphia in evaluation, eligibility determinations or IEP documents. (OSERS Dear Colleague Letter, 10/23/15) [85]

"The Office of Special Education and Rehabilitation Services (OSERS) has received communications from stakeholders, including parents, advocacy groups, and national disability organizations, who believe that State and local educational agencies (SEAs and LEAs) are reluctant to reference or use dyslexia, dyscalculia, and dysgraphia in evaluations, eligibility determinations, or in developing the individualized education program (IEP) under the IDEA.

"The purpose of this letter is to clarify that there is nothing in the IDEA that would prohibit the use of the terms dyslexia, dyscalculia, and dysgraphia in IDEA evaluation, eligibility determinations, or IEP documents."

. . .

"Under the IDEA and its implementing regulations "specific learning disability" is defined, in part, as "a disorder in one or more of the basic psychological processes involved in understanding or in using language, spoken or written, that may manifest itself in the imperfect ability to listen, think, speak, read, write, spell, or to do mathematical calculations, including conditions such as perceptual disabilities,

---

[84] http://www2.ed.gov/policy/speced/guid/idea/memosdcltrs/15-008269r-mi-lipsitt-statecomplaint-090915.pdf

[85] http://www2.ed.gov/policy/speced/guid/idea/memosdcltrs/guidance-on-dyslexia-10-2015.pdf

brain injury, minimal brain dysfunction, *dyslexia*, and developmental aphasia." See 20 U.S.C. §1401(30) and 34 CFR §300.8(c)(10) (emphasis added)." [86]

OSERS concluded:

> "OSERS further encourages States to review their policies, procedures, and practices to ensure that they do not prohibit the use of the terms dyslexia, dyscalculia, and dysgraphia in evaluations, eligibility, and IEP documents."

November 2015

U.S. Attorney's Office Reaches Agreement with Detroit Public Schools to Ensure Effective Communication for Parents Who Are Deaf and Hard of Hearing (Department of Justice news release 11/02/15) [87]

In a press release issued on November 2, 2015,, the U.S. Attorney's Office for the Eastern District of Michigan advised, "This settlement agreement resolves a complaint that Detroit Public Schools failed to provide a sign language interpreter to the deaf parent of a student enrolled in the district's family- centered Early Childhood Intervention program."

> "An Early Childhood Intervention (EI) program in Detroit provides services for infants and toddlers with developmental delays. Parental involvement is a key component of the program. The parent of a child who attended the EI program is deaf and could not participate in her child's education because the district refused to provide a sign language interpreter at teaching sessions.

> "The ADA requires that public entities, such as public schools, provide effective communication to all individuals with disabilities who seek to participate in or benefit from a school district's services, programs or activities—not just students. This can include parent participation in parent-teacher conferences, student registration, meetings, ceremonies, open houses, and field trips."

The link to Settlement Agreement Between the United States of America and the School District of the City of Detroit (Department of Justice, 11/2/15) is also in this footnote.[88]

Policy Guidance on FAPE: High Expectations and IEPs Aligned with Grade Level State Academic Content Standards (OSERS Dear Colleague Letter, 11/16/15)[89]

The Office of Special Education and Rehabilitative Services (OSERS) is concerned that "low expectations can lead to children with disabilities receiving less challenging

---

[86] In *Wrightslaw Special Education Law, 2nd Ed.* see pages 56 and 194 for the U.S.C. and CFR cites.

[87] https://www.justice.gov/usao-edmi/pr/us-attorneys-office-reaches-agreement-detroit-public-schools-ensure-effective

[88] http://www.ada.gov/detroit_sa.html

[89] http://www2.ed.gov/policy/speced/guid/idea/memosdcltrs/guidance-on-fape-11-17-2015.pdf

instruction that reflects below grade-level content standards, and thereby not learning what they need to succeed at the grade in which they are enrolled."

OSERS advised that children with disabilities who struggle to learn reading and math "can learn grade-level content and make significant academic progress" if their school provides "appropriate instruction, services, and supports."

The child's IEP Team must consider how the child's disability affects his ability to advance toward annual goals that are aligned with State content standards. Annual IEP goals must be aligned with State academic content standards for the grade in which the child is enrolled.

The IEP Team may consider the special education instruction provided by the school, the child's rate of academic growth, "and whether the child is on track to achieve grade-level proficiency within the year."

For example, if a child is performing below grade level, the IEP Team should consider annual goals to help "close the gap." "[T]he annual goals need not necessarily result in the child's reaching grade-level within the year covered by the IEP, but the goals should be sufficiently ambitious to help close the gap."

In the letter, OSEP used an example of a sixth grade child reading at the second grade level and the steps that are expected to be taken. OSEP suggested that "he should receive specialized instruction to improve his reading fluency. Based on the child's rate of growth during the previous school year, the IEP Team estimates that with appropriate specialized instruction the child could achieve an increase of at least 1.5 grade levels in reading fluency."

Destruction of Personally Identifiable Information (PII) - Letter to Julie J. Weatherly (OSEP Policy Letter, 11/23/15)[90]

Part B of IDEA requires school districts to inform parents of their right to request that the school destroy their child's Personally Identifiable Information (PII) when it is no longer needed to provide educational services to the child, and to actually destroy the PII at the request of the parents (but permits the maintenance of certain specific information).

The purpose of the destruction option is to allow parents to decide that records about a child's performance, abilities, and behavior, which may be stigmatizing and are highly personal, are not maintained after they are no longer needed for educational purposes.

This policy letter includes the definition of "personally identifiable" information.

Maintenance of effort (MOE) and Reducing LEA Expenditures on Special Education - Letter to Michael Lovato (OSEP Policy Letter, 11/23/15)[91]

This policy letter provides guidance regarding an exception to maintenance of effort (MOE). The LEA may not reduce the expenditure of funds below that spent the prior year,

---

[90] http://www2.ed.gov/policy/speced/guid/idea/memosdcltrs/15-010851-al-weatherly-records-to-clear.pdf

[91] http://www2.ed.gov/policy/speced/guid/idea/memosdcltrs/14-017166-nm-sea-lea-moe.pdf

however, there may be exceptions. Assume the school district contracted outside for speech language service provider at a cost of $100,000 per year and, the following year, hires a speech language service provider for $50,000. Depending on circumstances, the LEA may or may not take a "qualified deduction" in MOE. Various examples are provided in the policy letter.

Proportionate Share of Funds for Equitable Services Used as Settlement - Letter to Michael I. Inzelbuch (OSEP Policy Letter, 11/23/15)[92]

May a school district dedicate a portion of its proportionate share funds to be used as part of a settlement agreement without the "timely and meaningful consultation" required by the IDEA regulations?[93]

A school district has proposed a settlement agreement in which a student will withdraw from the district and enroll in the private school as a parentally placed student. Can the school district use part of their proportionate share funds to pay for services to that student?

Timely, meaningful consultation must occur before making any decisions that will affect parentally placed children. An LEA cannot unilaterally dedicate part of its proportionate share funds to carry out the terms of a settlement agreement with a student without complying with these requirements.

December 2015

Statute of Limitations to Request a Due Process Hearing: Letter to Perry Zirkel (OSEP Policy Letter, 12/09/15)[94]

If a State does not have an explicit time limitation to request a due process hearing, is the statute of limitations to file four years or two years?

OSEP noted, "The Court of Appeals for the Third Circuit addressed this question in *G.L. v. Ligonier Valley School District Authority*, 802 F.3d 601 (3d Cir. 2015). The Court requested that the Department submit an amicus curiae letter brief about the relationship between the two statutory provisions. The Department submitted a letter . . ."

"On September 22, 2015, the Third Circuit issued its decision, holding that both provisions reflect the same two-year deadline for filing a due process complaint after the date plaintiffs knew or should have known about the alleged violations (the 'KOSHK date')."

---

[92] http://www2.ed.gov/policy/speced/guid/idea/memosdcltrs/15-011136-nj-inzelbuch-equitable-services-11-10-15.pdf

[93] 34 CFR §300.134

[94] http://www2.ed.gov/policy/speced/guid/idea/memosdcltrs/14-000122-pa-zirkel-sol.pdf

News: ESEA (NCLB) Reauthorized as Every Student Succeeds Act (ESSA) (12/10/15)[95]

In December, Congress voted to reauthorize the Elementary and Secondary Education Act (ESSA) and gave the law a new name: "Every Student Succeeds Act" (ESSA).

On December 10, 2015, the President signed the Act into law. The complete ESSA statute is on our Wrightslaw.com website.[96]

In 1965, Congress enacted the ESSA as the Elementary and Secondary Education Act to address the inequality of educational opportunities for underprivileged children.

Congress reauthorized the Individuals with Disabilities Education Act in 2004. The IDEA is overdue for reauthorization but has languished in legal limbo for years. The reauthorization of ESSA may open the path to reauthorization of IDEA.

Expedited Due Process Hearings – Letter to Colleen A. Snyder (OSEP Policy Letter, 12/13/15)[97]

Is an expedited due process hearing mandatory when a due process complaint is submitted in a discipline matter? Can a parent or school district (LEA) request that a hearing not be subject to the expedited due process timeline?

If a parent or school district requests a due process hearing in a disciplinary matter, the State educational agency (SEA) or school district (LEA) must arrange "for an expedited hearing, which must occur within **20 school days** of the date that the due process request is filed." The purpose of expediting a due process hearing of a disciplinary decision "is to ensure that the matter is resolved promptly and the child's educational program is not adversely affected by undue delays."

"There is no provision . . . that would give a hearing officer . . . authority to extend the timeline for issuing this determination at the request of a party to the expedited due process hearing."

In Summation

In this chapter, you learned about news and developments in the world of special education. In the next chapter, you'll dive into decisions from Courts of Appeals - with a little help from the Table of Decisions that begins on page 42.

---

[95] http://www.ed.gov/essa?src=rn

[96] http://www.wrightslaw.com/essa/essa.391pages.pdf

[97] http://www2.ed.gov/policy/speced/guid/idea/memosdcltrs/15-012744-ca-snyder-exdueprocess-clearance.pdf

Chapter 3. Decisions in IDEA Cases by Courts of Appeal in 2015

The Table of Decisions that begins on the next page is a seven-page list of decisions in IDEA cases by Courts of Appeals from January 1 through December 31, 2015. The decisions are in chronological order and include the date of the decision, circuit, author of the decision if known, an abbreviated "style of the case," key issues addressed in the ruling, outcome, and prevailing party.

As you review the decisions in the Table, you will see that the cases have two links. Each case has a bookmark in the "style of the case," i.e., *CW v. Capistrano* or *Stanek v. St. Charles Sch Dist.* that will take you to a more comprehensive discussion of that case. The second link will take you to the full text of the decision on Google Scholar.

Some cases do not include the name of the Judge who authored the decision. These cases are usually identified by the Court as "Per Curiam" decisions and are delivered as rulings by the Court, acting collectively, and not by a specific judge.

Cases in which IDEA 2004 was not an issue and roughly half a dozen "Summary" decisions by Courts of Appeal that included minimal detail and law are not included in ***Wrightslaw: Special Education Legal Developments and Cases 2015.***

Do you remember your Circuit?

It's time to turn this page.

Table 2. Decisions by Courts of Appeals in IDEA Cases (2015)

Date	Circuit & Judge	Short Style	Key Issues & Concepts in Decision
2/5/2015	5th Cir. Smith	*Fort Bend Ind Sch Dist v. Douglas A.*	Tuition reimbursement, residential placement must be for educational reasons. Outcome: LEA prevailed.
https://scholar.google.com/scholar_case?case=18007600932749054579			
3/2/2015	9th Cir. Wardlaw	*CW v. Capistrano*	IEE, reverse due process, frivolous, improper purpose, attorney's fees sought by school district. Outcome: Parent prevailed.
https://scholar.google.com/scholar_case?case=9526138798984490734			
3/2/2015	9th Cir.	*Lainey C. v. Hawaii Dept of Ed*	Failure to exhaust, failure to raise issues at due process hearing, mainstreaming, landmark "*Rachel Holland*" case. Outcome: LEA prevailed.
https://scholar.google.com/scholar_case?case=3960772488057198668			
3/6/2015	3rd Cir. Jordan	*WD v. Watchung Hills*	Tuition reimbursement, 10-day notice by parent, enrollment in private school prior to public school's proposed IEP. Outcome: LEA prevailed.
https://scholar.google.com/scholar_case?case=16607831868387394460			
3/16/2015	9th Cir. Watford	*Fairfield-Suisun + Yolo v. CA DOE*	Two school districts v state DOE with LEAs attacking SEA complaint process. Statutory authority, state administrative complaint. Outcome: SEA prevailed.
https://scholar.google.com/scholar_case?case=6561397870687548013			
3/19/2015	2nd Cir.	*RB v. NYC Dept of Ed*	Tuition reimbursement, procedural violation, standard for review on appeal. Outcome: LEA prevailed.
https://scholar.google.com/scholar_case?case=7838237322092296939			

4/9/2015	7th Cir. Wood	*Stanek v. St. Charles Sch Dist*	§ 1983 for IDEA violation, individual employee liability for violation of IDEA, § 504, ADA, retaliation, discrimination, *Winkelman* issue. Outcome: Parents prevailed.
https://scholar.google.com/scholar_case?case=6381745525167116786			
4/15/2015	6th Cir. Moore	*Wenk v. O'Reilly*	False child abuse report by school, retaliation, qualified immunity, § 1983, constitutional violation, First Amendment, protected speech. Outcome: Parents prevailed.
https://scholar.google.com/scholar_case?case=2798491115432530666			
4/28/2015	11th Cir.	*Laura A. v. Limestone Bd Ed*	"Rule of Construction" requirement for exhaustion, due process hearing for 504 / ADA case, constitutional violations. Outcome: LEA prevailed
https://scholar.google.com/scholar_case?case=16561292144139584781			
5/8/2015	2nd Cir.	*EH v. NYC Dept Ed*	Autism, appropriate educational methodology, "DIR / Floortime," tuition reimbursement. Outcome: Parent prevailed.
https://scholar.google.com/scholar_case?case=2815104725065432557			
5/11/2015	7th Cir.	*Foster v. Amandla Charter Sch &* Chicago	Charter school, failure to evaluate, *Winkelman* issue, compensatory education. Outcome: Parent prevailed.
https://scholar.google.com/scholar_case?case=12819653988981168391			
5/26/2015	DC Cir. Tatel	*Boose v. DC Pub Sch*	Child find, failure to evaluate, compensatory education, moot. Outcome: Parent prevailed.
https://scholar.google.com/scholar_case?case=3735014752034740375			
6/1/2015	9th Cir.	*DB v. Santa Monica-Malibu Sch Dist*	IEP meeting w/o parent, procedural violation, parental participation, *Doug C.* case. Outcome: Parent prevailed.
https://scholar.google.com/scholar_case?case=828727817058144693			

Special Education Legal Developments & Cases 2015

6/5/2015	9th Cir. Clifton	*Sam K. v. Hawaii DOE*	Predetermination of placement, deprivation of meaningful parental participation, tuition reimbursement, SOL, hourly rate of attorney's fees, Outcome: Parent prevailed.
https://scholar.google.com/scholar_case?case=12029727086156008750			
6/11/2015	3rd Cir.	*HL v. Downingtown Sch Dist.*	Tuition reimbursement, LRE, inclusion, *Oberti case*, public and private program not appropriate. Outcome: LEA prevailed.
https://scholar.google.com/scholar_case?case=12764944789766682326			
6/12/2015	6th Cir. Rogers	*Fry v. Napoleon Comm Sch*	Service dog case under 504 / ADA. Due process hearing for Section 504, ADA violation, failure to exhaust, exhaustion required. Outcome: LEA prevailed. Petition for Cert pending.
https://scholar.google.com/scholar_case?case=8326079484204683753			
6/12/2015	6th Cir. Merritt	*Oakstone Sch. v. Williams*	Attorney's fees to LEA, attorney's fees to parent, frivolous, sanctions. Outcome: Parent, parent's attorney, LEA's attorney not sanctioned, not required to pay fees of other side.
https://scholar.google.com/scholar_case?case=851050078348606932			
6/26/2015	2nd Cir. Jacobs	*Doe v. East Lyme Bd. of Ed.*	Autism, compensatory ed, Orton-Gillingham, stay-put, tuition reimbursement. Outcome: LEA prevailed.
https://scholar.google.com/scholar_case?case=10532577435221403225			
6/26/2015	DC Cir. Wilkins	*Price v. DC Pub. Sch.*	Statutory cap of $90/hour for attorneys' fees struck. Outcome: Parent's attorney prevailed.
https://scholar.google.com/scholar_case?case=13214863408909626234			
7/2/2015	11th Cir. Tjoflat	*TP v. Bryan County Sch Dist*	IEE, reverse due process, case now moot. Outcome: LEA prevailed.
https://scholar.google.com/scholar_case?case=15740402807001322381			

7/6/2015	9th Cir. Callahan	*Meridian Sch Dist v. DA*	Four cases, IEE, injunction, SOL for attorney's fees, parent as prevailing party, whether child is "a child with a disability." Outcome: Parent prevailed on IEE; SEA prevailed on all other issues.
https://scholar.google.com/scholar_case?case=14805098815993068140			
7/10/2015	DC Cir. Henderson	*Eley v. DC Pub Sch*	Attorney's fees, matrix, prevailing market rate. Outcome: Award reduced, remanded back to recalculate.
https://scholar.google.com/scholar_case?case=11596699457041133534			
7/10/2015	DC Cir. Tatel	*Leggett v. DC Pub Sch*	Pro se parent, tuition reimbursement for private day v. private boarding, failure to complete IEP prior to beginning of school year. Outcome: Parent prevailed.
https://scholar.google.com/scholar_case?case=17124127189470382064			
7/14/2015	DC Cir. Tatel	*McAllister v. DC Pub Sch*	Attorney's fees for lay advocate v. paralegal. Outcome: lay advocate employed by attorney was an expert, thus no attorney's fees. LEA prevailed.
https://scholar.google.com/scholar_case?case=9539323013127177504			
07/15/15	2nd Cir.	*MO v. NYC Dept Ed*	Tuition reimbursement for unilateral placement; IEP adequate as written & pro-vided FAPE. Outcome: LEA prevailed
https://scholar.google.com/scholar_case?case=15034548072126496014			
7/31/2015	9th Cir. Clifton	*TB v. San Diego*	Plaintiff's rejection of settlement offer justified, attorney's fees awarded. Outcome: Parent prevailed.
http://scholar.google.com/scholar_case?case=8025171964440764885			
8/7/2015	8th Cir. Beam	*Sneitzer v. Iowa*	Tuition reimbursement denied - insufficient evidence to support. Outcome: LEA prevailed.
https://scholar.google.com/scholar_case?case=12896591552882956423			

8/25/2015	10th Cir.	*Endrew v. Douglas Sch Dist*	Tuition reimbursement denied, argued new definition of educational benefit. Outcome: LEA prevailed.
https://scholar.google.com/scholar_case?case=12338798572806686443			

9/2/2015	8th Cir. Beam	*BS v. Anoka Hennepin*	ALJ restricted time for witness examination. Outcome: LEA prevailed.
https://scholar.google.com/scholar_case?case=8734083776530172638			

9/10/2015	3rd Cir. Fisher	*DM v. NJ DOE*	SEA attempted to close down hybrid private spec ed school with joint classes with regular ed students. Stay-put issue. Outcome: SEA lost.
https://scholar.google.com/scholar_case?case=3492767239545860893			

9/15/2015	10th Cir. Gorsuch	*AF v. Espanola*	Settled IDEA claim, litigated ADA / 504, case dismissed, failed to exhaust. Outcome: Parent did not prevail.
https://scholar.google.com/scholar_case?case=9651538761292785355			

9/22/2015	3rd Cir. Krause	*GL v. Ligonier*	Two year Statute of Limitations does not limit equitable remedy to two years. Outcome: Parent prevailed.
https://scholar.google.com/scholar_case?case=12010940798039221978			

10/19/2015	4th Cir. Motz	*OS v. Fairfax*	Parents sought to create new definition of educational benefit; *Rowley* case. Outcome: LEA prevailed.
https://scholar.google.com/scholar_case?case=5074524769153538743			

10/29/2015	3rd Cir. Ambro	*JF v. Byram*	Comparable IEP question; child in private school with tuition paid by school district. Parent moved, new district not required to fund private placement. Outcome: LEA prevailed.
https://scholar.google.com/scholar_case?case=1440389023842185540			

10/30/2015	11th Cir.	*Phyllene v. Huntsville*	School denied FAPE by failing to fully evaluate child in all areas. Outcome: Parent prevailed.
https://scholar.google.com/scholar_case?case=13695525979808795195			
11/10/2015	5th Cir. Higginson	*DG v. New Caney*	Timeline for attorney fee petition based on state law. Outcome: Parent prevailed.
https://scholar.google.com/scholar_case?case=13426815846253109814			
11/10/2015	10th Cir. McHugh	*Carroll v. Lawton*	Child abuse by teacher, 504 + ADA case dismissed, failed to exhaust administrative remedies. Outcome: LEA prevailed.
https://scholar.google.com/scholar_case?case=15546509366247355334			
11/17/2015	6th Cir. Cook	*QW v. Fayette*	Eligibility, autism did not adversely affect educational performance, child not eligible for IEP. Outcome: LEA prevailed.
https://scholar.google.com/scholar_case?case=6056373496203312158			
11/17/2015	9th Cir. Du	*IR v. Los Angeles*	School failed to request Due Process when parent disagreed with portion of IEP per CA law. Outcome: Parent prevailed.
https://scholar.google.com/scholar_case?case=8565309195291905938			
11/18/2015	2nd Cir.	*DAB v. NYC Bd. Ed.*	Tuition reimbursement, public school IEP was procedurally and substantively adequate. Deference to findings of state review officer appropriate. No evidence to support Section 504 claims that DOE discriminated against child. Outcome: LEA prevailed.
https://scholar.google.com/scholar_case?case=10768052050977072795			
12/22/2015	3rd Cir. Fuentes	*MS v. Marple*	Child with disability under Sec. 504, no IEP, sued under 504 / ADA. Case dismissed, parents failed to exhaust administrative remedies under IDEA. Outcome: LEA prevailed.
https://scholar.google.com/scholar_case?case=7149981657124821842			

12/30/2015	2nd Cir.	*BP v. NYC Dept. Ed.*	Reimbursement for private education expenses, appropriateness of proposed placement, placement school implement IEP, issues not raised in due process complaint cannot be introduced later. Outcome: LEA prevailed.
https://scholar.google.com/scholar_case?case=7748265229141495564			
12/30/2015	11th Cir.	*AL v. Jackson Co. Sch. Bd.*	IDEA claims re: IEE, Extended School Year (ESY), parent participation, Fourth Amendment claim (daily searches at alternative school where child received ESY), 504 / ADA discrimination & retaliation claims. 4th amendment claim reversed & remanded; LEA prevailed on all other issues.
https://scholar.google.com/scholar_case?case=17789868402871551476			

Fort Bend Ind Sch Dist v. Douglas A.
779 F.3d 959 (5th Cir. 2015)
February 2, 2015

In this Indiana case, the parent sought reimbursement of tuition for a residential placement. The parent prevailed at the District Court level but lost before the Court of Appeals. As the Court explained:

"Fort Bend Independent School District ("FBISD") challenges a ruling holding it responsible for reimbursing the parents of one of its former students, Z.A., for his residential placement under the Individuals with Disabilities Education Act ("IDEA"), 20 U.S.C. § 1400 et seq. Because the district court erred in concluding that the residential placement was appropriate, we reverse and render judgment for FBISD."

"Whether a placement will help the student is properly considered under the first criterion of the *Michael Z.* test. A court must determine whether the student was placed in the residential program for educational reasons; that he actually will realize educational benefits is irrelevant under that factor if those benefits are incidental to the reasons for placing him."

"For the RedCliff placement, the evidence uniformly supports the conclusion that the parents placed Z.A. for non-educational purposes; indeed, the court found that he was placed at RedCliff because his parents were concerned that he would make another attempt at suicide and because he had a drug problem. There is, however, no evidence showing that they then enrolled Z.A. at CALO for educational reasons."

CW v. v. Capistrano
784 F.3d. 956 (9th Cir. 2015)
March 2, 2015

CW appealed the district court's award of attorney's fees to the school district.

CW is described as having "cerebral palsy, a ventriculoperitoneal shunt, a heart murmur ... and low cognitive ability."

After completing the required triennial evaluation of CW, the team determined that she continued to be eligible for special education services under the "Other Health Impairment" category. The team recommended that she receive an occupational therapy evaluation of her gross and fine motor development.

The occupational therapist's evaluation "made several recommendations for goals, modifications and accommodations" but "did not recommend whether any direct OT services were needed." When the parent was presented with the OT assessment at the next IEP meeting, she became upset and "expressed shock."

On January 25 2011, the parent "requested an independent educational evaluation (IEE) for occupational therapy based on her disagreement with the occupational therapy portion" of the IEP. On February 23, the school district refused to grant this request. On March 4 2011, the district requested a due process hearing against the parent. The issues were described as:

"(1) whether the OT assessment was appropriate; and

(2) whether the District committed a procedural IDEA violation by delaying unnecessarily in filing its due process complaint."

"The ALJ concluded that the OT assessment was administered properly pursuant to the correct test manual and in compliance with the statutory requirements. The ALJ also concluded that the forty days between the IEE request and the filing of the Due Process complaint was not unnecessary delay."

Thereafter the communications between the attorneys became embittered and CW filed an appeal in the U.S. District Court. The Court upheld the ALJ's decision and also "awarded $94,602.34 in attorney's and $2,058.21 in costs. The district court found that each of the claims was "frivolous, unreasonable, and without foundation." Further, the court concluded that these claims were brought by K.S. for the improper purpose of "harassment, unnecessary delay, and needlessly increasing litigation costs," exposing K.S. to potential personal liability for the fees.

CW appealed the district court's award of attorney's fees to the school district.

The Ninth Circuit held that the violations of IDEA and 504 were not frivolous, that the case was not brought for an "improper purpose" and reversed, partially. The Court noted, "Where a plaintiff has asserted both frivolous and non-frivolous claims, a prevailing defendant may recover attorney's fees under § 1988 for the time attributable to defending against solely the frivolous claims."

The Court referred the remaining issue "to the Appellate Commissioner for a determination of which fees are attributable solely to litigating the frivolous § 1983 claim and ADA claims in this case, subject to reconsideration by this Court, and affirm the award of attorney's fees against K.S.'s attorneys to that extent."

Judge Reinhardt wrote a vigorous dissent to the Appellate Commissioner, stating, "I would hope that on rehearing the majority, which has otherwise issued an excellent opinion that is fully consistent with the letter and spirit of the IDEA, will reconsider and delete the few offending paragraphs affirming sanctions — paragraphs that sound so jarring and contrary a note to the rest of its disposition."

On April 9, 2015, the court entered a separate order noting Judges Wardlaw and Callahan voted to deny a rehearing, Judge Reinhardt voted to grant it. The full panel of the Ninth Circuit declined to hear the case en banc.

Wrightslaw Note: Several California law school spec education clinics participated in this case.

Lainey C. v. Hawaii Dept. of Ed.
9th Cir. - March 2, 2015

Lainey C. is a very short "not for publication" Memorandum in which the court of appeals quickly disposed of the appeal from the district court.

This case involved a 12 year old with high functioning autism whose parent requested a 1:1 aide to help with socialization. In earlier proceedings, an Administrative Hearing Officer ruled against the parents. The District Court upheld this decision.

The Court affirmed a behavioral specialist's opinion that providing an aide might cause the child to be less independent and more socially isolated.

The Court noted: "Lainey has also not shown that her IEP was not reasonably calculated to address her educational needs. First, Lainey's IEP did not fail to address her socialization needs. Relying on the testimony of a behavioral specialist, both the AHO and the district court determined that Lainey did not require one-to-one aid. Lainey has not shown that this finding of fact is clearly erroneous."

On appeal, the parents raised five new arguments about the inadequacy of the child's IEP that had not been raised at the DP Hearing.

"This court has held that an argument not raised in an administrative complaint or due process hearing is not exhausted and cannot be raised for the first time on appeal to the district court."

With regard to mainstreaming, the court noted that when analyzing a mainstreaming decision, courts are to consider the four factors enumerated in *Sacramento City School Dist. v. Rachel H.*, 14 F.3d 1398 (9th Cir. 1994) and that "Lainey did not cite to, or provide any analysis of, these factors."

The District Court's ruling against parents was affirmed.

WD v. Watchung Hills Regional
3rd Cir. - March 6, 2015

A New Jersey parent was concerned about his child's transition from middle school to high school. In June 2012, the parent obtained a private evaluation on the child. The evaluator concluded that the child's needs were not being met at the public school.

On July 10, the parent submitted an application for his son to attend The Forman School. On August 7, the boy was accepted. One week later, the parent signed the enrollment agreement and paid the tuition.

On August 24, the parent's attorney sent a letter to Watchung Hills seeking tuition reimbursement for The Forman School. On September 5, the parent's attorney sent the private evaluation to the district. On September 5, the district held an IEP meeting. When district staff learned that the child was already enrolled at the private school, they terminated the IEP meeting.

The parent requested a due process hearing on the issue of tuition reimbursement, lost, then appealed to the US District Court. That court upheld the adverse ruling by the Administrative Law Judge. The parent appealed to the Third Circuit, which upheld the prior rulings.

As the Court explained, "W.D. did not follow the notice requirements set out in the statute and thus the District Court did not err in denying his reimbursement claim. W.D. notified Watchung Hills of his intent to remove his son from the school district less than 10 business days prior to W.C.D. starting orientation at The Forman School, and several days after W.D. had enrolled W.C.D. in that school and paid the first year's tuition.

We, and other courts, have previously denied reimbursement when, as in this instance, the parent fails to satisfy the 'obligation to cooperate and assist in the formulation of an IEP and ... to timely notify the District of [the] intent to seek private school tuition reimbursement ... IDEA was not intended to fund private school tuition for the children of parents who have not first given the public school a good faith opportunity to meet its obligations."

The parent had complained about the school district's failure to provide information about the specific methodologies that would be used with his child and information about the qualifications of the child's teacher.

The Court held, "As noted in the *Federal Register*, 'nothing in [the IDEA]... requires an IEP to include specific instructional methodologies ... The Department [of Education]'s long-standing position on including instructional methodologies in a child's IEP is that it is an IEP Team's decision.' Similarly, with some limited exceptions not applicable here, 'nothing in [the IDEA] ... require[s] schools ... to provide parents with information about the qualification of their child's teachers and other service providers.'"

In a footnote, the Court emphasized that the parent signed the enrollment agreement on August 13 and paid the full tuition on August 16, prior to submitting the required ten business day notice.

Wrightslaw Note - These actions sabotaged their case. When I had an active practice and represented parents who were considering a private placement, I always had them write a letter to the private school noting that admission was subject to whether the public school provided an appropriate IEP. The parents advised the private school that if the public school provided an appropriate IEP, they were prepared to forfeit their deposit. Private evaluations were always provided to the school district promptly upon receipt.

Fairfield-Suisun + Yolo v. CA DOE 780 F.3d 968 (9ᵗʰ Cir. 2015) **March 16, 2015**

In separate actions, two school districts (LEAs) sued the California Department of Education (DOE) about their administrative complaint procedures.

As background, in both cases, the DOE ruled in favor of parents. In one case on a request to reconsider, the DOE reversed and ruled in favor of the LEA and then, after a subsequent request for reconsideration from the parent, reversed again and ruled in favor of the parent. The LEA claimed that the law permits one reconsideration.

In the other case, the State DOE placed the burden of proof on the LEA, not on the parent, and "considered conduct outside the one year statute of limitations imposed by 34 CFR SS 300.153(c)."

In both actions, "the district courts dismissed the actions with prejudice on the ground that Congress did not grant school districts a right to sue state agencies for violating procedural requirements imposed by the IDEA."

The Ninth Circuit consolidated the two cases and upheld and affirmed the rulings of the district courts. In dismissing the case and ruling on behalf of the California Dept. of Education, the court noted that "IDEA's procedural protections are 'intended to safeguard the rights of disabled children and their parents . . .'" and that there is no statutory authority in IDEA that permits an LEA to sue an SEA.

RB v. NYC Dept. of Ed. **2nd Cir. - March 19, 2015**

In this New York case, the parents of a child with autism sued for tuition reimbursement. After the parents lost before an Impartial Hearing Officer (IHO) and the State Review Officer (SRO), they appealed to U.S. District Court. After the District Court upheld the SRO's decision, the parents appealed to the Second Circuit. That Court upheld the District Court's decision.

The Court of Appeals wrote, "development of the IEP was not unblemished. We agree with the district court and the SRO that the IEP should have provided for parent counseling and training. But . . . this omission, although a procedural violation, did not deny the student a free appropriate public education."

The Second Circuit described the process of reviewing decisions by SROs and District Courts. "[T]he responsibility for determining whether a challenged IEP will provide a child with an appropriate public education rests in the first instance with administrative hearing and review officers, and we defer to their expertise on education policy . . . Deference is particularly appropriate when the state officer's review `has been thorough and careful,' but still we do not 'simply rubber stamp administrative decisions.'"

Stanek v. St. Charles Sch. Dist. 783 F.3d 634 (7ᵗʰ Cir. 2015) **April 9, 2015**

This Illinois case began as a reverse due process hearing. When the parents refused to provide consent for a re-evaluation, the LEA requested a due process hearing. The parents filed "a cross-complaint alleging that the District and several teachers and administrators had denied educational services to Matthew and had discriminated and retaliated against him and his parents. Mediation proved fruitless, and eventually the hearing officer dismissed the Staneks' complaint for failure to comply with prehearing requirements."

The parents appealed this adverse decision to state court, alleging violations of IDEA, Section 504 and the ADA. The school district removed the case to federal court and "promptly filed a motion to dismiss" which was granted by the District Court.

Matthew and his parents appealed to the Seventh Circuit. Judge Wood opened with this statement:

"Matthew Stanek, now 20 years old, is autistic. While he was a high school student in the St. Charles Community Unit School District #303 ('the District'), he received special-education services. Although he is now in college, he and his parents, Bogdan and Sandra Stanek, still have some accounts to settle with the District. Invoking their rights under the federal Constitution and several laws, they have sued both the District and various administrators and teachers for failing to provide necessary educational services to Matthew before his graduation. The district court dismissed the action against Bogdan and Sandra on the theory that they lack standing to sue. Although Matthew did have standing, the court dismissed his case for failure to sue an appropriate party. We conclude that some of these rulings do not withstand scrutiny. We therefore vacate the dismissal in part and remand for further proceedings."

The court noted that the Complaint filed in federal court alleged that: "Without the measures specified in the IEP [extra time + study guides], Matthew started receiving failing grades in the AP and honors classes, but he refused to drop them. Concerned, Bogdan and Sandra scheduled a meeting at the school to discuss the situation. That only made matters worse: some of Matthew's teachers began neglecting to record good grades he had earned and recording grades lower than those he actually had earned. These teachers also refused to give Matthew credit for completed work and ignored his questions about his assignments. Matthew became distressed and anxious, and he began to suffer headaches and nausea and to miss school. His parents were forced to hire a tutor to compensate for the periods when he was out of school or too distraught to learn. School administrators also began ignoring Bogdan and Sandra's requests for Matthew's educational records and refused to meet with them."

In regard to the 504 and ADA discrimination claims, the treatment by his teachers "caused

him extreme anxiety, loss of self-esteem, emotional stress, and physical pain, and prevented him from attending school every day, resulting in lost educational opportunity. At this stage in the litigation, that is sufficient."

The parents "also sufficiently allege that the District retaliated against them by shutting them out of the special-education process, in violation of the Rehabilitation Act and the ADA...[T]he school froze them out after their requests. This is enough."

The Court's decision includes a lengthy discussion about using § 1983 to pursue remedies under IDEA, noting that the circuits are split on this issue, and concluding, "We think it best to refrain from deciding at this time whether any of the Staneks might be able to seek recourse under § 1983. It is not clear that resolution of this question will make any practical difference in this case."

With regard to personal liability of a school employee for violation of IDEA, the court noted, "We draw the line, however, at the IDEA claims, which should have gone forward at this stage. We have not found a decision from any circuit holding that individual school employees cannot be personally liable for violating IDEA."

The Court of Appeals vacated the District Court decision, remanding it for further proceedings.

Wenk v. O'Reilly
783 F.3d 585 (6th Cir. 2015)
April 15, 2015

Ohio parents, Peter and Robin Wenk, sued Nancy Schott, Director of Pupil Services, in U.S. District Court because she made false reports to protective services. Schott claimed that she had qualified immunity from suit, in part because, as a school official she is a mandatory reporter of child abuse. When the District Court denied her the protection of qualified immunity, she appealed to the Sixth Circuit.

Judge Moore opened the opinion with this summary: "Plaintiffs Peter Wenk and Robin Wenk, parents of an intellectually-disabled 17-

year-old girl, brought suit under 42 U.S.C. § 1983 against various defendants, including Nancy Schott, the Director of Pupil Services at their daughter's school. The Wenks allege that Schott filed a child abuse report about Peter Wenk in retaliation for the Wenks' advocacy to change their daughter's educational plan, and Schott therefore violated their First Amendment rights. The district court denied Schott qualified immunity, and Schott now appeals . . ."

The Wenks had to convince the court that Schott's conduct was retaliation for a constitutionally protected activity, i.e., protected speech (advocacy) on behalf of their daughter and that Schott did not have immunity.

The Court explained that three elements must be met before a constitutional violation of the First Amendment occurs:

"We analyze First Amendment retaliation claims under a burden-shifting framework. 'A plaintiff must first make a prima facie case of retaliation,' which has three elements:

(1) he engaged in constitutionally protected speech or conduct;

(2) an adverse action was taken against him that would deter a person of ordinary firmness from continuing to engage in that conduct; [and]

(3) there is a causal connection between elements one and two — that is, the adverse action was motivated at least in part by his protected conduct."

"Schott does not contest that the Wenks' advocacy about M.W.'s educational plan is protected activity. Rather, Schott argues that the Wenks cannot establish the second and third elements of their prima facie case."

"Schott's child abuse report constitutes an adverse action. We have held twice that reports of child abuse 'would deter a person of ordinary firmness from continuing to engage' in protected conduct under the First Amendment and therefore such reports can constitute adverse action."

"The Wenks have established that Schott 'was motivated at least in part by [the Wenks'] protected conduct' in filing the child abuse report."

Concluding that there was a constitutional violation, the Court added, "Schott claims that all of the information that she reported to FCCS came from Hayes and Sidon." However, in discovery depositions, special education teachers Sidon and Hayes both "dispute that they told Schott much of the information that Schott reported to FCCS or that some of the events Schott reported ever occurred."

"In sum, we hold that the Wenks' right to be free from retaliation for exercising their First Amendment rights was clearly established at the time of this case, and that a reasonable official in Schott's position would have understood that filing a child abuse report in bad faith violated the Wenks' rights."

Expanding on the issue of false child abuse reports by school officials, the Court wrote, "A reasonable official in Schott's position would have understood that what she did violated the Wenks' right to be free from retaliation for exercising their First Amendment rights. Our decision in *Jenkins*, decided in 2008, made clear that school officials can be liable if they make reports of child abuse to retaliate against parents for exercising their First Amendment rights. 513 F.3d at 588-89. Although the report in *Jenkins* was false, the heart of a First Amendment retaliation claim, which we have reaffirmed numerous times before 2011, is that '[a]n act taken in retaliation for the exercise of a constitutionally protected right is actionable under § 1983 even if the act, when taken for a different reason, would have been proper.' *Bloch*, 156 F.3d at 681-82. Under this rule, it is clear that the distinction between a completely false report and a partially false report does not matter."

Laura A. v. Limestone Bd. Ed.
11th Cir. - April 28, 2015

In Alabama, Laura A, the grandmother and "next friend" of J.O. requested a due process hearing to contest a finding that J.O. was no longer eligible for special education. While the record is not clear, it appears that the grandmother lost at due process. On appeal to U.S. District Court, she alleged Section 504 violations. In her letter requesting a due process hearing, she did not allege violations of Section 504. Pursuant to a Motion for summary judgment filed by the LEA, the District Court dismissed the case.

"On appeal, [to the Eleventh Circuit] Ms. A. argues that the district court erred in concluding that she failed to exhaust administrative remedies for her § 504 claim. After thorough review, we affirm."

The Court explained that "Under the plain language of IDEA, before a civil action may be brought under § 504, 'the procedures under subsections (f) and (g) [of § 1415] shall be exhausted to the same extent as would be required had the action been brought under this subchapter.' 20 U.S.C. § 1415(l) ... Thus, whether Ms. A.'s claims are brought pursuant to IDEA, the ADA, § 504 or the Constitution, they must first be exhausted in state administrative proceedings. Indeed, it would subvert the purposes of the exhaustion requirement to allow exhaustion of an IDEA claim to also suffice for a Rehabilitation Act claim seeking some of the same relief, when the claims have different elements, the proof required under both statutes is different, and the Rehabilitation Act claim was not addressed at all during the administrative proceedings. . ."

Since Ms. A. did not seek a due process hearing for her § 504 claims, she cannot now pursue a civil action for those claims."

The court noted that "the purposes behind the exhaustion requirement include:

(1) permitting the exercise of agency discretion and expertise on issues requiring these characteristics;

(2) allowing the full development of technical issues and a factual record prior to court review;

(3) preventing deliberate disregard and circumvention of agency procedures established by Congress; and

(4) avoiding unnecessary judicial decisions by giving the agency the first opportunity to correct any error").

Wrightslaw Note: In this circuit, it seems that if you have a constitutional violation for which no relief can be granted by the Hearing Officer or Administrative Law Judge for a child with an IEP, you must exhaust administrative remedies, i.e., request a special education due process hearing. See ***Wrightslaw: Special Education Law 2nd Ed.***, at page 123 and footnote 181 and the discussion about 20 U.S.C. § 1415(l).

However, in a number of special education cases where dollar damages were sought, through "artful pleading," the failure to exhaust was not a bar to the case proceeding. Be aware of all case law in your District Court and Court of Appeals as it evolves. See also the 6th Circuit decision in *Laura A.* below and the pending Petition for Certiorari filed with the Supreme Court in *Fry v. Napoleon.*

EH v. NYC Dept. Ed.
2nd Cir. - May 8, 2015

EH v. NYC is an educational methodology case.

Pursuant to a special education due process hearing for the 2010-2011 school year, the NYC Dept. of Ed paid the tuition for M.K, a child with autism, to attend the Rebecca School "which uses a teaching methodology known as the 'DIR/Floortime' method."

On February 11 2011, while M.K. was enrolled in the Rebecca School, the NYC Dept. of Ed convened an IEP meeting for the 2011-2012 school year. While the proposed IEP included goals that "came directly from a report created by the Rebecca School," the placement was not at the Rebecca School. The parent requested a due process hearing to seek prospective tuition at the Rebecca School for the 2011-2012 school year. "After a three-day hearing, the IHO agreed that M.K. had been denied a FAPE and ordered the DOE to fund M.K.'s tuition. The DOE appealed to a state review officer ('SRO') who, on July 25, 2012, reversed the IHO after concluding that the IEP was 'sufficient to address the student's demonstrated needs and [was] designed to enable him to make progress.'

E.H. then filed suit in U. S. District Court for the Southern District of New York, seeking reversal of the SRO's decision. The parties cross-moved for summary judgment and, on March 21, 2014, the district court affirmed. This appeal [to the Second Circuit] followed."

As the Court explained, "We review a district court's grant of summary judgment in an IDEA case de novo ... But although we 'engage in an independent review of the administrative record,' we must give 'due weight' to the state administrative decisions, 'mindful that the judiciary generally lacks the specialized knowledge and experience necessary to resolve persistent and difficult questions of educational policy.' This often means deferring to the 'final decision of the state authorities, even where the reviewing authority disagrees with the hearing officer.' Only if the SRO's decision is 'insufficiently reasoned to merit ... deference,' may we disregard it in favor of the IHO's decision."

In the body of the opinion, the Court strikes several arguments raised by the parents about the inadequacy of the IEP, the proposed classroom, and the behavioral intervention plan (BIP). However, the Court concluded the opinion with a discussion of "DIR/Floor time" and appropriate educational methodology.

The court explained that neither the IHO nor the SRO determined "whether the 'DIR/Floor time' methodology was necessary to implement the goals in the IEP. The IHO noted that the IEP adopts the Rebecca School's goals without requiring the use of the 'DIR/Floor time' method, but did not assess whether the IEP is 'likely to produce progress' toward M.K.'s goals even without that teaching methodology ... On appeal, the SRO also failed to evaluate whether M.K. could progress without 'DIR/Floor time.' Instead, it held that the IHO should not have addressed the methodology issue because E.H. failed to raise the issue in the due process complaint ... But that decision was incorrect — E.H.'s due process complaint contained at least three objections to the IEP's failure to adopt the 'DIR/Floor time' methodology. And contrary to the district court's decision, the SRO's general conclusion that the IEP was 'sufficient to

address the student's demonstrated needs,' is no replacement for a direct evaluation of the evidence on teaching methodology. As we explained in M.H., a 'failure to consider any of the evidence regarding ... methodology ... is precisely the type of determination to which courts need not defer.'"

"We therefore vacate the district court's decision and remand so that the district court can direct the SRO to determine, in the first instance, whether the DOE denied M.K. a FAPE by adopting the Rebecca School's goals without also adopting the 'DIR/Floor time' methodology ... If the SRO concludes that the DOE denied M.K. a FAPE, either the SRO or district court must also address whether the Rebecca School is an appropriate alternative placement and whether equitable considerations favor reimbursement."

Wrightslaw Note: This decision relied heavily on *M.H. v. N.Y.C. Dept of Educ.*, 685 F.3d 217 (2d Cir. 2012)

Foster v. Amandla Charter Sch. & Chicago Bd Ed
7th Cir. - May 11, 2015

This is a failure to evaluate or "child find" case.

In January 2010, via a written note, Illinois parent Debra Foster requested that Amandla Charter School evaluate her daughter for an IEP. The charter school did not evaluate the child for an IEP but instead initiated a 504 Plan.

"A year later, the parent again requested that the school evaluate her daughter for an IEP. Not two years after her original request did the charter school staff explain that she had to sign a consent form before the child could be evaluated. The school failed to provide the consent form. In that same month, the parent wrote to request a "Full IEP" and "case study."

Another year passed before the charter school scheduled an IEP meeting "which Foster, after attending, derided as a sham. At that point Foster requested a due-process hearing."

At the due process hearing, Amandla staff "testified that they had known the girl was struggling in classes and at some point had a § 504 plan. Foster requested that the school district provide speech and language evaluations, reimbursement for the evaluations she had procured, a new school placement, and 'compensatory education' to include various reading, speech, and language services."

"The hearing officer determined that, since at least November 2011, the school had possessed 'ample evidence' that Foster's daughter needed special-education services but, he speculated, her paperwork likely 'fell through the cracks.'"

"The hearing officer noted that the student should receive 'compensatory education' for the period dating back to March 2012, by which time, he thought, Amandla should have evaluated the girl and implemented an IEP. He concluded that, since that time, the girl had made significant gains during her sessions with the speech and language pathologist but still required 'an additional 25 intensive sessions' to achieve the level that 'she would have occupied but for the denial' of special-education services under IDEA."

Since a new school year was starting when the Hearing Officer's Decision was issued, "Foster enrolled her daughter at a different public charter school. The girl, who is still a minor, was evaluated and given an IEP for her high school program at the new school."

"Amandla and the Board of Education of the City of Chicago did nothing to challenge the hearing officer's decision, but Foster did. Foster, purporting to represent her daughter as well as herself, filed this action alleging that Amandla and the Board had violated IDEA by not providing the girl with a free appropriate public education."

The court noted that "Foster's federal complaint seeks reimbursement for the cost of her daughter's sessions with the speech and language pathologist which . . . is not among the relief she requested from the hearing officer. It followed, the court reasoned, that Foster was not aggrieved by the hearing officer's decision. And since that decision did give Foster other

relief, the court added, she has no claim under IDEA."

"On the defendants' motions, the district court dismissed the action with the explanation that without an attorney Foster cannot litigate claims belonging to her daughter and that she fails to state a claim of her own."

The Court provided an analysis of *Winkelman* on whether a parent can represent their child before the district court. The Court noted, "...Foster acknowledges the distinction, but she reads *Winkelman* as holding that a pro se parent can litigate a minor child's claims under IDEA. That reading is incorrect. *Winkelman* confirms that parents of a child with a learning disability have their own enforceable rights under IDEA, but the decision specifically leaves open the question whether IDEA allows a parent to litigate the child's claims without counsel. And we have repeatedly held that the rule prohibiting a non-lawyer from representing another person extends to a parent attempting to represent her minor child pro se."

While ruling against the parent on the *Winkelman* issue, the Court addressed issues relating to "compensatory education" and the Court's power to grant equitable relief, including "prospective equitable relief." The Court of Appeals vacated the "compensatory education" and "equitable relief" portions of the district Court's order and remanded the case back to the district court to determine the appropriate compensatory education and relief.

Boose v. DC Pub. School
786 F.3d 1054 (DC Cir. 2015)
May 26, 2015

"In this case arising under the Individuals with Disabilities Education Act, 20 U.S.C. § 1400 *et seq.*, plaintiff seeks an order requiring the District of Columbia Public Schools to provide her son with compensatory education to make up for the period during which the school system, allegedly in violation of the statute, failed to identify and evaluate him. The school system responded with an individualized education plan that is, by all accounts, adequate to keep the child on track going forward, and the district court dismissed the suit as moot. But because the district court failed to address whether A.G. was entitled to compensatory education—a remedy that remains available— we reverse."

"If a school district fails to satisfy its 'child-find' duty or to offer the student an appropriate IEP, and if that failure affects the child's education, then the district has necessarily denied the student a free appropriate public education . . . And when a school district denies a child a FAPE, the courts have 'broad discretion' to fashion an appropriate remedy . . . That equitable authority, this court has held, must include the power to order 'compensatory education'—that is, education services designed to make up for past deficiencies in a child's program . . . because the Supreme Court has held that IEPs need do no more than provide 'some educational benefit' going forward . . . an education plan conforming to that standard will speak only to 'the child's present abilities . . . Unlike compensatory education, therefore, an IEP 'carries no guarantee of undoing damage done by prior violations,' id., and that plan alone cannot take the place of adequate compensatory education."

"But as DCPS concedes, that IEP included no education to compensate for the period— kindergarten through the first few weeks of first grade during which A.G. allegedly lacked an appropriate education plan."

"IEPs are forward looking and intended to 'conform to . . . [a] standard that looks to the child's present abilities,' whereas compensatory education is meant to 'make up for prior deficiencies.'"

"Because Boose expressly requested compensatory education, and because DCPS has never offered it, 'the complaint present[s us] with a live controversy,' and Boose's case is not moot."

The district court decision was reversed and remanded back to determine compensatory ed.

DB v. Santa Monica-Malibu Sch. Dist.
9th Cir. - June 1, 2015

"Santa Monica-Malibu Unified School District appeals the district court's final order awarding D.B. reimbursement for the cost of tuition at the Westview School for the 2010-11 school year, related educational expenses and attorney's fees and costs. We have jurisdiction under 28 U.S.C. § 1291, and we affirm."

"The district court properly concluded the District's failure to include D.B.'s parents at the June 8 meeting was a procedural violation of the IDEA. The IDEA's implementing regulations require that parents participate in meetings concerning the formulation of an Individualized Education Program (IEP) and the educational placement of their child. See 34 C.F.R. §300.501(b). An agency can make a decision without the parents only if it is unable to obtain their participation, which was not the case here."

"The district court properly concluded the procedural violation denied D.B. a free appropriate public education in the 2010-11 school year. See *Doug C.*, 720 F.3d at 1044-47; *Amanda J. ex rel. Annette J. v. Clark Cnty. Sch. Dist.*, 267 F.3d 877, 892 (9th Cir 2001). 'Procedural violations that interfere with parental participation in the IEP formulation process undermine the very essence of the IDEA.' *Amanda J.*, 267 F.3d at 892.

"Proceeding without the child's parents cannot be justified by the scheduling unavailability of District employees; the attendance of parents at IEP Team meetings 'must take priority over other members' attendance.'"

The district court's decision was affirmed.

Sam K. v. Hawaii DOE
788 F.3d 1033 (9ᵗʰ Cir. 2015)
June 5, 2015

In Hawaii, the school district (LEA) is also the also SEA so the Hawaii Dept. of Ed provides special education services. As a result of prior litigation and a subsequent settlement agreement, Sam K. was enrolled in Loveland Academy, a private school, for several years at the expense of the state Dept. of Education. Hawaii DOE proposed an IEP for the 2010-2011 year that placed the child in a public school program. The parents did not accept the proposed IEP.

In Hawaii, if parents unilaterally place their child into a private program and seek tuition reimbursement and if the Hawaii DOE refuses to pay for the private program, the parents must request a due process hearing on the reimbursement issue within 180 days after the placement.

The primary issue in this case was whether the placement at Loveland Academy was a unilateral placement, which triggers the 180-day statute of limitations, or a "bilateral" placement with a SOL of two years.

On most issues, the Hearing Officer ruled in favor of the parents, finding that the public school placement was "predetermined," was inappropriate, and was "potentially disastrous" to Sam. The HO determined that Loveland was appropriate.

The Hearing Officer also found that continuation of enrollment at Loveland was a unilateral placement, triggering the 180-day SOL, and denied reimbursement.

The parents appealed to the District Court. The District Court found that the Loveland placement was "bilateral," not "unilateral," reversed, and found that the parents were entitled to reimbursement.

The Hawaii DOE appealed the district court's decision to the Court of Appeals. Hawaii DOE based their appeal on the SOL issue, not on the IEP and predetermination issues. The parents cross-appealed the award of attorney's fees "contending that the hourly rate used in calculating the award was too low."

The Court of Appeals affirmed the district court's decision about the parent's entitlement to reimbursement, found that the 180-day SOL was not applicable, but upheld the $275 hourly rate award of attorney's fees.

Judge Rawlinson wrote a strong dissent asserting that the placement was "unilateral."

HL v. Downingtown Sch. Dist.
3d Cir. - June 11, 2015

Pennsylvania parents rejected an IEP for their child with LD and placed the child into Kimberton, a private school. Per a settlement agreement, the public school paid the child's tuition for the first year while the intermediate unit provided supplemental reading and writing instruction. In the IEP for the next year, the school district offered an IEP a public school with additional language arts instruction. The child's parents rejected this IEP and filed for due process, seeking tuition reimbursement.

The HO and the District Court held that the public school 'failed to adequately consider greater inclusion' but also opined that Kimberton was not an appropriate program. In finding that the public school program was not appropriate, the circuit court discussed "inclusion," "LRE," "least restrictive environment" and the *Oberti* case. The court concluded that the school district's shortcomings did not make the Kimberton program appropriate as it had deficiencies and the child's progress at Kimberton "was minimal."

The District Court's denial of tuition reimbursement was upheld because the private program, like the public program, was not appropriate.

Fry v. Napoleon Comm. Sch. Dist.
788 F.3d 622 (6TH Cir. 2015)
June 12, 2015

This Michigan case is about a young child's use of a service dog at school. After a trial period with the dog at school, the school district refused to allow the service dog to return the next year.

After years of stalled negotiations, the parents sued the school, its principal, and the school district, alleging violations of the ADA and the Rehabilitation Act and state disability law. The district court granted the defendants' motion to dismiss under Fed. R. Civ. P. 12(c) on the grounds that because the Frys' claims necessarily implicated E.F.'s IEP, the IDEA's exhaustion provision required the Frys to exhaust IDEA administrative procedures prior to bringing suit under the ADA and Rehabilitation Act. The Frys appeal, arguing that the IDEA exhaustion provision does not apply because they do not seek relief provided by IDEA procedures. But because the specific injuries the Frys allege are essentially educational, they are exactly the sort of injuries the IDEA aims to prevent, and therefore the IDEA's exhaustion requirement applies to the Frys' claims."

"E.F., the daughter of Stacy and Brent Fry, was born with spastic quadriplegic cerebral palsy, which significantly impairs her motor skills and mobility. In 2008, E.F. was prescribed a service dog. Over the course of the next year, E.F. obtained and trained with a specially trained service dog, a hybrid goldendoodle named Wonder. Wonder assists E.F. by increasing her mobility and assisting with physical tasks such as using the toilet and retrieving dropped items. At the time this dispute arose, E.F. could not handle Wonder on her own, but at some point in the future, she would be able to. In October 2009, when Wonder's training was complete, her school, Ezra Eby Elementary School, refused permission for Wonder to accompany E.F. at school. There was already an IEP in place for E.F. for the 2009-2010 school year that included a human aide providing one-on-one support. In a specially convened IEP meeting in January

2010, school administrators confirmed the decision to prohibit Wonder, reasoning in part that Wonder would not be able to provide any support the human aide could not provide. In April 2010, the school agreed to a trial period, to last until the end of the school year, during which E.F. could bring Wonder to school. During this trial period, however, Wonder was not at all times permitted to be with E.F. or to perform some functions for which he had been trained. At the end of the trial period, the school informed the Frys that Wonder would not be permitted to attend school with E.F. in the coming school year."

"The Frys then began homeschooling E.F. and filed a complaint with the Office of Civil Rights at the Department of Education under the ADA and § 504 of the Rehabilitation Act. Two years later, in May 2012, the Office of Civil Rights found that the school's refusal to permit Wonder to attend with E.F. was a violation of the ADA. At that time, without accepting the factual or legal conclusions of the Office of Civil Rights, the school agreed to permit E.F. to attend school with Wonder starting in fall 2012. However, the Frys decided to enroll E.F. in a school in a different district where they encountered no opposition to Wonder's attending school with E.F."

Several months later, pursuant to Section 504 of the Rehabilitation Act and Title II of the Americans with Disabilities Act, the Frys filed suit against the school district seeking damages.

The parents did not request a special education due process hearing under IDEA. The school district filed a motion to dismiss asserting that the parents' failure to exhaust their administrative remedies under IDEA mandated dismissal.

"On January 10, 2014, the district court granted the defendants' motion to dismiss pursuant to Rule 12(c), finding that the IDEA's exhaustion requirements applied to the Frys' claims and dismissing them without prejudice. The court noted that although the Frys did not specifically allege any flaw in E.F.'s IEP, if she were permitted to attend school with Wonder, that document would almost certainly have to be modified in order to articulate the policies and practices that would apply to the dog."

The court of appeals upheld the dismissal by the district court and wrote extensively about the requirement to exhaust administrative remedies:

"We have held that exhaustion is not required when the injuries alleged by the plaintiffs do not 'relate to the provision of a FAPE [free appropriate public education]' as defined by the IDEA, and when they cannot 'be remedied through the administrative process' created by that statute. When they do relate to the provision of the child's education and can be remedied through IDEA procedures, waiving the exhaustion requirement would prevent state and local educational agencies from addressing problems they specialize in addressing and require courts to evaluate claims about educational harms that may be difficult for them to analyze without the benefit of an administrative record."

The court noted that the parents, via a due process hearing, could have appealed the determination of the IEP team.

"Although the Frys seek money damages, a remedy unavailable under the IDEA, rather than an injunction, this does not in itself excuse the exhaustion requirement . . . Otherwise, plaintiffs could evade the exhaustion requirement simply by appending a claim for damages."

"It is true that IDEA procedures, which could at best require Ezra Eby Elementary to permit Wonder to accompany E.F. at school, would not at present be effective in resolving the Frys' dispute. First, E.F. no longer attends Ezra Eby Elementary, and her current school and school district permit Wonder to accompany her. Second, before the Frys decided to transfer E.F., the defendants settled the Frys' ADA complaint before the Department of Education's Office of Civil Rights and agreed to permit Wonder to accompany E.F. at school; IDEA procedures could not have produced a substantially better outcome."

The court of appeals affirmed the dismissal since the Fry's did not exhaust their administrative remedies and pursue a special education due process hearing.

Judge Daughtrey wrote a dissent, below, that was nearly as long as the majority's decision: "The disability discrimination at issue is a text-book example of the harms that Section 504 and the ADA were designed to prevent, and the claims should not have been dismissed essentially because the victim of the discrimination was a school-aged child."

"The majority proposes to affirm the district court's order dismissing this civil rights action alleging violation of Section 504 of the Rehabilitation Act and Title II of the Americans with Disabilities Act (ADA), based on its conclusion that 'the specific injuries the [plaintiffs] allege are essentially educational' and, therefore, subject to administrative exhaustion under an entirely separate statute, the Individuals with Disabilities Act (IDEA). Because I conclude to the contrary that the claim here is non-educational in nature and that the IDEA's exhaustion provision was improperly invoked by the district court, I respectfully dissent. Moreover, even if the accommodation sought could be considered 'educational,' the fact that school policy would permit a 'guide dog' on campus, but not a certified 'service dog,' suggests why an attempt at exhaustion of administrative remedies would be futile in this case and should be excused."

Wrightslaw Note: The Fry's appealed to the Supreme Court. The original complaint, decisions from the district court and Court of Appeals, and Petition for Certiorari filed with the Supreme Court are on the Wrightslaw site. In January 2016, the Court asked the Solicitor General to write a brief about whether the Court should hear this case.

Oakstone Comm. Sch. v. Williams + Zraik
6th Cir. - Judge Merritt
June 12, 2015

In this Ohio case, on "December 2010, Defendant Cassandra Williams (represented by Defendant Thomas R. Zraik) filed an administrative complaint with the Ohio Department of Education alleging that Oakstone had denied her daughter a 'free appropriate public education.' Following several days of public hearings, an Impartial Hearing Officer denied the complaint after finding that the child had in fact made both academic and behavioral progress while enrolled at Oakstone. As the prevailing party, Oakstone (represented by Shank) subsequently filed this case in district court to recover attorney's fees under the Education Act's fee-shifting provision."

The opening paragraph from the Court of Appeals decision states, "What began as a case about a child's education has needlessly devolved into a dispute about attorney's fees and unjustified sanctions. After prevailing in an administrative claim filed by the Defendant parent and her lawyer . . . Oakstone Community School filed this separate action for attorney's fees under the Education Act's fee-shifting provision. See 20 U.S.C. §1415(i)(3)(B)(i)."

This section allows a prevailing school district to recover reasonable attorney's fees 'against the attorney of a parent who files [an administrative] complaint . . . that is frivolous, unreasonable, or without foundation.' Id. Additionally, a prevailing school district can recover from a parent—or her attorney—if the administrative action was brought 'for an improper purpose, such as to harass, to cause unnecessary delay, or to needlessly increase the cost of litigation.' Id. Because Oakstone sought legal fees on both grounds, the complaint included both the parent (Williams) and her attorney (Zraik)."

The Court then noted that "An acrimonious course of litigation ensued in which Defendants (Williams and her attorney, Zraik) repeatedly threatened to pursue sanctions against Oakstone's counsel, Appellant S. Adele Shank, for nearly everything she did. Defendants were ultimately successful, and the district court imposed $7,500 in personal sanctions against [school board attorney] Shank on three separate grounds . . ."

At the District Court level, after Shank "filed this case in district court to recover attorney's fees . . . Defendants' counsel immediately threatened her with Rule 11 sanctions because they believed this case was "frivolous." When Shank amended the complaint, Defendants moved to dismiss and sent her a second letter—again threatening to pursue Rule 11 sanctions unless she "dismiss[ed] the Amended Complaint immediately."

"The district court later granted Defendants' Motion to Dismiss [neither Williams nor Zraik were liable for attorneys fees] after finding that the original administrative hearing was not brought for an improper purpose." In response to the Motion for Sanctions and an award of attorneys' fees against Shank, the district court then sanctioned Shank in the amount of $7,500, presumably to be paid to Zraik. However, Shank appealed to the Court of Appeals.

The Court of Appeals analyzed each instance of Shank's alleged misconduct and found that the District Court abused its discretion in awarding $7,500 in attorneys' fees and sanctions against Shank and reversed the order of sanctions.

In essence, after the parents and their counsel lost at the DP Hearing, Oakstone Community School and attorney Shank asserted that the hearing was frivolous and filed suit in District Court to recover their attorneys' fees. Although the district court case was dismissed, it boomeranged against Shank in that she was sanctioned by the District Court. This decision was reversed by the Court of Appeals. The Circuit Court decision included a comprehensive discussion about frivolous, improper purpose, sanctions, etc.

Doe v. East Lyme
2nd Cir. - June 26, 2015

In this Connecticut case, by agreement, a child with autism was enrolled in a private school located in another school district at public expense. The parents were dissatisfied with this private school so, after two years, they placed child into another private school. The parents agreed to pay the tuition and East Lyme agreed to pay for some related services, including PT/OT, and speech therapy along with Orton-Gillingham therapy.

For the next school year, the district offered an IEP with placement in a public school. Parents rejected that IEP and requested that the district pay for the private school and related services. East Lyme refused and stopped paying for the related services. Parents requested a DP Hearing seeking tuition reimbursement for the private school, related services, stay-put for those prior related services and continuation of related services provided by school district.

After parents rejected the IEP, litigation continued. East Lyme did not offer an IEP for subsequent years. The parents asserted that the public school was liable for those years.

The HO and district court concluded that East Lyme's IEP was appropriate and also found that the private school was not appropriate. The district court found that the failure to offer an IEP for the interim years was a denial of FAPE but the parent was not entitled to relief because the private school was not appropriate. The Court of Appeals agreed.

However the court noted, "It is undisputed that the Board refused to pay for the services described in that IEP during the pendency of administrative and judicial proceedings. The Board thus violated the stay-put provision."

"The Board argues that the Parent was required to administratively exhaust her stay-put claim. The Board is wrong: 'an action alleging violation of the stay-put provision falls within one, if not more, of the enumerated exceptions to' the IDEA's exhaustion requirement . . . Applying the exhaustion requirement to stay-put claims

would create a loop of marathon proceedings . . ."

However, the court noted that "the Parent filed her due process complaint almost a full year after the impasse was reached. In any event, the statute is clear that the Board's obligation to provide stay-put services was not triggered until the Parent's administrative complaint was filed."

While the district court awarded reimbursement for the tutoring expenses incurred during the violation of the stay-put period, the circuit court remanded the case back on that issue alone:

"We affirm the judgment in most respects, but vacate the award of reimbursement and remand the case for further proceedings. We hold that the appropriate equitable relief for a stay-put violation is reimbursement or compensatory education (or both) for the full value of services that the educational agency was required to fund, not the (lesser) value of services the Parent was able to afford. We further hold that an educational agency's obligation to maintain stay-put placement is triggered when an administrative due process proceeding is initiated, not when an impasse is reached."

The case was remanded back to U.S. District Court to evaluate the stay-put violation. The denial of tuition reimbursement to the parents by the district court was affirmed by the Court of Appeals.

Price + Weems v. DC Pub. Sch.
792 F.3d 112 (DC Cir. 2015)
June 26, 2015

Price is one of several cases about attorney's fees that were decided by the D.C. Circuit in 2015.

"Appellants in this case successfully pursued administrative proceedings against the District of Columbia Public Schools ("DCPS") to vindicate rights to a free appropriate public education under the Individuals with Disabilities Education Act ("IDEA")."

"Following success on the merits in administrative proceedings before DCPS, Appellants sought reimbursement for their attorney fees at $250 per hour. DCPS refused to pay more than $90 per hour, which is the statutory rate at which attorneys are paid by the D.C. Courts under the D.C. Criminal Justice Act. See D.C. Code § 11-2604(a). To challenge that refusal, Appellants brought this suit in District Court under 20 U.S.C. § 1415(i)(2) seeking reimbursement at what they contend is the applicable market-based *Laffey* rate of $505 per hour."

"The District Court granted summary judgment in favor of DCPS, denying Appellants any recovery beyond the $90 per hour they already had received from DCPS. See *Price v. District of Columbia*, 61 F. Supp. 3d 135 (D.D.C. 2014). Appellants timely noticed this appeal."

The court of appeals, in reversing the district court and striking the DC statutory cap of $90 an hour, noted that: "First, as a factual matter, the constructive terms of representation that Mr. Bergeron accepted were to receive the benefit of IDEA fee shifting from DCPS if he was successful while retaining a fallback of $90 per hour compensation from the D.C. Courts if his client did not 'prevail.' That he undertook the representations in this case on those terms does not demonstrate he would have been willing to accept the work on the open market for a fixed rate of $90 per hour. Second, even if Mr. Bergeron accepted these assignments from the Superior Court and would have performed them at a $90 rate because of the public interest nature of the case, his clients remain entitled to fee shifting at the prevailing rate. Our Court has held that the prevailing market rate method applies to 'attorneys who practice privately and for profit but at reduced rates reflecting non-economic goals'. . . [F]ee shifting is "to be calculated according to the prevailing market rates in the relevant community, regardless of whether plaintiff is represented by private or nonprofit counsel."

The Court struck down DC's statutory cap on attorneys' fees, noting, "The $90 per hour statutory compensation rate in the D.C. Criminal

Justice Act did not preempt the prevailing-rate determination required in IDEA fee shifting . . ."

The court reversed and remanded back for an award of fees based on rates prevailing in the community.

T.P. v. Bryan County Sch. Dist. 792 F.3d 1284 (11ᵗʰ Cir. 2015) July 2, 2015

This Georgia case is about IEEs. As the Court explained, "This appeal arises under the Individuals with Disabilities Education Act ("IDEA") . . . [and] concerns the request by the parents of T.P., a child with autism and speech and language disabilities, that their son's school district pay for an independent educational evaluation ("IEE") of T.P. to determine his educational needs. T.P.'s parents requested this IEE because, they claimed, the evaluation the district conducted more than two years prior was deficient. The school district denied the parents' request, informing them that it would first conduct its own reevaluation of T.P., and that if they disagreed with the results, they could then seek an IEE."

"The school district and parents independently filed requests for a hearing before a state Administrative Law Judge ("ALJ"). The parents claimed, among other things, that the school district had inappropriately denied their request for a publicly funded IEE, and they requested an order requiring the district to pay for an IEE of their son. The district requested a declaration that its denial was appropriate because the IDEA's two-year statute of limitations to enforce the right to a publicly funded IEE had run. It also requested the ALJ to order the parents to consent to a reevaluation of T.P."

"In separate orders, the ALJ ruled that the statute of limitations had run and ordered the parents to consent to a reevaluation.

The parents filed a civil action in federal district court to review the ALJ's ruling. On the school district's motion, the District Court dismissed the parents' complaint, holding that the parents' request in the state administrative proceeding was time-barred. It did not address the ALJ's order requiring the parents to consent to a reevaluation.

The child was evaluated by the school district in 2010, IEPs over the next two years were agreed upon. However "In November 2012, the Parents — now contending that the 2010 evaluation was 'improper'—requested the District to pay for an IEE. After several weeks of communication with the Parents, the District denied their request. The District explained that the request was untimely, as the IDEA's two-year statute of limitations had run . . . Alternatively, the District contended that the request was invalid, as it was not based on a disagreement with the 2010 evaluation."

"Despite rejecting the Parents' request for an IEE at public expense, the District acknowledged the Parents' concerns and asked the Parents to allow it to reevaluate T.P. A triennial reevaluation of T.P. was not due until August 2013 . . . The District informed the Parents that if they were dissatisfied with the reevaluation, they could then request an IEE at public expense. The Parents, however, would not consent to a District-conducted reevaluation; they wanted an IEE at public expense." In an unusual twist, the court of appeals dismissed the case as "moot."

"Because a reevaluation of T.P. is due, the relief the Parents seek — an order directing the District to pay for an IEE — will no longer redress the procedural injury they allege. Were we now to direct the District Court to order the District to pay for an IEE, it would not empower the Parents to participate in the IEP process. Thus, the Parents lack a legally cognizable interest in the outcome of the appeal, and their appeal is moot."

Meridian Sch. Dist. v. D. A.
792 F.3d 1054 (9th Cir. 2015)
July 6, 2015

This Idaho case involved three separate appeals, Nos. 13-35329 and 13-36200, styled as *Meridian Jt. Sch. Dist. v. D.A.*, reported as one decision, and No. 14-35081 styled as *D.A v. Meridian Jt. Sch. Dist.*, and reported as a short, separate "Not for Publication" decision. Decisions that involved all three cases were published on July 6, 2015. A fourth case between the parties included an eight-day jury trial. The jury ruled in favor of the LEA. *Meridian Sch. Dist. v. D.A.*

Matthew had an IEP for several years. After a re-evaluation, he was found no longer eligible for an IEP and instead had a 504 Plan. In his freshman year, he set fire to his room at home and was incarcerated in a juvenile facility for about a year and a half. Prior to his release, his parents requested that the school evaluate him again and that he receive an IEP.

The school district refused, noting that the evaluation done on Matthew while he was incarcerated showed that his disabilities (some LD and Asperger) did not adversely affect educational performance.

After numerous meetings, the parents requested an Independent Educational Evaluation (IEE), which the school district refused. The school district then asked for a due process hearing and an order confirming that an IEE was not necessary.

"The matter was assigned to Special Education Hearing Officer Guy Price (HO Price), who conducted three weeks of hearings on two issues: (1) '[i]s the Student entitled to an Independent Educational Evaluation, as requested by his attorney on January 17, 2011'; and (2) '[d]oes the Student qualify for special education pursuant to the eligibility criteria set forth in the IDEA and the *Idaho Special Education Manual.*'"

"In a June 6, 2011 decision, HO Price found that MSD had failed to conduct an appropriate evaluation, held that Matthew was entitled to an IEE at public expense, and declined to rule on whether he qualified for special education services, stating that such a determination would be premature prior to the completion of an appropriate evaluation."

"In July 2011, MSD filed an action in the District Court of Idaho seeking judicial review of HO Price's decision. On May 23, 2012, the district court issued an order granting the Parents' motion to enjoin Matthew's graduation from high school. In March 2013, the district court issued an order affirming HO Price's decision and dismissing MSD's appeal. On April 17, 2013, MSD filed a timely notice of appeal (Appeal No. 13-35329). Thereafter, the district court conducted further proceedings on the Parents' request for attorneys' fees. On October 16, 2013, the district court entered an order granting the Parents attorneys' fees. The final judgment was entered on November 25, 2013, and MSD filed a timely notice of appeal from the award of attorneys' fees on December 20, 2013 (Appeal No. 13-36200)."

In the preceding paragraph, the court provided the docket numbers for the primary decision in this case regarding the two appeals by the LEA, one related to the IEE and the high school graduation injunction, and the other about the award of attorney's fees. In the next paragraph the court discusses the other case No. 14-35081 as follows:

"Meanwhile, pursuant to HO Price's directive, an IEE was prepared for Matthew and submitted to MSD in September 2011. MSD proceeded to evaluate Matthew's eligibility for special education services under the IDEA. In January 2012, the Parents filed a request for a due process hearing alleging that MSD had not timely evaluated Matthew. In February 2012, MSD determined that Matthew was not eligible for special education. The Parents then filed a second due process complaint challenging that ruling. The two due process complaints were consolidated into one case that was heard by the Hearing Officer. HO Litteneker conducted 10 days of hearings over two months before issuing a decision on July 5, 2012, holding that Matthew was not entitled to special education services under the IDEA. The Parents then filed a complaint with the District Court, seeking review of HO Litteneker's decision. On January

6, 2014, the District Court issued a memorandum decision and order affirming HO Litteneker's decision that Matthew was not entitled to special education services. The Parents filed an appeal from that decision."

In the third case, after completion of the IEE, the school district found that Matthew was not eligible for an IEP. After a ten day due process hearing, the HO found that Matthew was not eligible for an IEP. On appeal to the district court, that finding was upheld. On the parent's subsequent appeal to the Ninth Circuit, the district court's decision that Matthew was not entitled to an IEP was upheld.

All the while, the parents filed a fourth case filed in district court, alleging that their son, was bullied in public school because of his disability. A quote from that case reported in Federal Rules Decision (F.R.D) notes that, "According to the parents, the student was relentlessly bullied verbally and physically and was called names, such as 'retard' during gym and had his clothes stolen."

As a side note, the Ninth Circuit mentioned that case:

"In addition, the Parents filed another action arising from the same background that is not before us. In February 2011, the Parents initiated administrative proceedings under the Rehabilitation Act and in March 2011, initiated an action alleging that MSD and BSD had violated Matthew's rights under the Americans with Disabilities Act (ADA). *D.A. v. Meridian Joint Sch. Dist. No. 2*, 289 F.R.D. 614, 620 (D. Idaho 2013). That action was ultimately resolved in an eight-day trial in the summer of 2013. The jury answered no to the special verdict question "was Matthew denied a free and appropriate public education by the Meridian School District."

There was no appeal from that July 31, 2013 jury verdict.

The court of appeals then focused on the issues of this case: the IEE, the injunction, and the award of attorney's fees to the parents.

"We conclude that the hearing officer, as well as the district court, carefully and thoroughly reviewed all the evidence and we also find that the evidence supports the conclusion that MSD's refusal to prepare an IEE when Matthew reentered high school was unreasonable. It was proper for the district court to credit HO Price's discussion of witness testimony that highlighted deficiencies in the BSD evaluation. Both the hearing officer and the district court were careful to note that neither was determining whether Matthew was entitled to special education services under the IDEA. Rather, they concluded that the evidence presented did not establish that he did not need such services. Their determinations are entitled to deference, but even on a de novo review we would affirm."

Affirming the District Court's decision that the school district should have provided an IEE, the Court then addressed the timing of the parent's request for an award of attorney's fees. The Court explained that IDEA does not provide a clear timeline or statute of limitations affecting the time to file an attorney fee request after a successful due process hearing.

"In the district court, MSD argued that the request was untimely because the applicable limitations period was either 14 or 42 days, and both periods had expired. The Parents asserted that the 90-day limitations period for appealing an adverse decision from a due process hearing under the IDEA applied to claims for attorneys' fees. The district court disagreed with both parties."

The court of appeals provided an extensive list of cases and discussed various rulings on this issue, and concluded that:

"Faced with an existing circuit split, we agree with the position taken by the district court. As set forth by the district court in *Ostby*, and consistent with the spirit of our decision in *Dreher*, we conclude that a request for attorneys' fees under the IDEA is more analogous to an independent claim than an ancillary proceeding. The fact that the hearing officer may not award attorneys' fees weighs in favor of holding that a request for attorneys' fees filed in the district court is not ancillary to the judicial review of the administrative decision. Moreover, the longer time period promotes the purposes of the IDEA. Indeed, the adoption of the state law limitations period for

judicial review of administrative agency decisions might lead to the anomalous result that the party that prevailed before the hearing officer would have to decide whether to file an action seeking attorneys' fees before the party that lost before the hearing officer decided whether to seek judicial review. Accordingly, we affirm the district court's determination that the Parents' request for attorneys' fees was timely filed under the most analogous state statute of limitations."

In a footnote, the Court noted, "This appears to be the three-year statute of limitations for statutory liability actions. *Idaho Code* § 5-218(1). But see *Henderson v. State*, 715 P.2d 978, 981 (Idaho 1986) (holding "42 U.S.C. § 1983 actions in Idaho must now meet the two-year Idaho statute of limitations for personal injury actions"). We need not decide this issue of state law as the Parents' request for attorneys' fees was timely under either state statute."

The court explained that for parents to have a right to attorney's fees, they must be prevailing parties. The court held that they were the prevailing parties. However, the court explained that the IDEA attorney fee statute permits fees "to a prevailing party who is the parent of a child with a disability."

It was determined that Matthew is not a child with a disability under IDEA, only a child with a disability under 504 and ADA.

"MSD reasons that because Matthew has not been determined to need special education services, the Parents are not eligible for an award of attorneys' fees pursuant to §1415(i)(3)(B)(i)(I)."

"The Fifth Circuit adopted this approach in *T.B. v. Bryan Independent School District*, 628 F.3d 240 (5th Cir. 2010), relying, in part, on an unpublished opinion by the Third Circuit, *D.S. v. Neptune Township Board of Education*, 264 F. App'x. 186 (3rd Cir. 2008), which was factually similar to Matthew's case."

In discussing the unpublished *Neptune* case, "The court rejected the suggestion that the fee-shifting provision should apply to children 'merely suspected of having a disability.'"

"The district court worried that MSD's interpretation would discourage parents from invoking their rights under the IDEA and create an incentive for schools to take an adversarial position early in the identification and evaluation process without fear of being liable for attorneys' fees."

"We appreciate the district court's concerns, but agree with the Fifth Circuit that we are bound by the clear language in the IDEA limiting the award of attorneys' fees to parents of a "child with a disability," defined as a child determined to need special education services."

"Accordingly, we vacate the district court's award of attorneys' fees."

With regard to the injunction, the court noted: "We agree that the district court had jurisdiction to consider the request for an injunction, and that the Parents did not have to show irreparable harm."

"Nonetheless, we question whether the district court should have issued the injunction in the first place, and we now vacate the injunction ... Whatever benefit that might have flowed from the injunction would appear to have been exhausted, and oral argument did not reveal any salient grounds for maintaining the injunction. Accordingly, we hereby vacate the injunction prohibiting Matthew's graduation from high school."

The court concluded, "We appreciate the concerns that underlie the parties' positions, and they have informed our disposition of these appeals. Pursuant to the applicable standards of review we conclude that: (1) the district court and the hearing officer reasonably determined that Matthew was entitled to an IEE at public expense; (2) the Parents' request for attorneys' fees is more analogous to an independent claim than an ancillary proceeding and thus was timely filed; (3) by procuring an IEE at public expense, the Parents were 'prevailing parties' as that term has been defined in *Hensley*, 461 U.S. at 433, and *Van Duyn*, 502 F.3d at 825; (4) because the plain language of the IDEA limits awards of attorneys' fees pursuant to 20 U.S.C. §1415(i)(3)(B)(i)(I) to instances in which the child has been determined to need special education services, and Matthew had not been found to need such services, the Parents are not eligible for an award of attorneys' fees under the IDEA; and (5) the injunction preventing Matthew's graduation from high school must be lifted ... we vacate the district court's award of attorneys' fees and its injunction preventing Matthew from graduating."

"AFFIRMED in part, REVERSED in part, and VACATED in part."

Eley v. DC Pub. Sch.
793 F.3d 97 (DC Cir. 2015)
July 10, 2015

"After Wilma Eley prevailed in her lawsuit against the District of Columbia (District) alleging a violation of the Individuals with Disabilities Education Act (IDEA), 20 U.S.C. §§ 1400 et seq., the district court awarded her $62,225 in attorneys' fees and costs for approximately one hundred hours of work. [$622.25/hour] Although the District lodged a variety of challenges to the award in the district court, its sole objection on appeal is to the prevailing market rate that court used in its calculation. Specifically, the District argues that the district court abused its discretion when it adopted Eley's proposed fee matrix, setting the prevailing market rate for her lawyer's services well beyond the next highest hourly rate used by district courts in IDEA litigation. For the reasons set forth below, we vacate the district court's fee award and remand."

"Here, the District no longer challenges the hours Eley's lawyer spent litigating her IDEA case, and the IDEA prohibits application of any 'bonus or multiplier,' 20 U.S.C. §1415(i)(3)(C). Accordingly, we move to the second prong of the SOCM analysis—the reasonable hourly rate. Whether an hourly rate is reasonable turns on three sub-elements:

(1) 'the attorney['s] billing practices,'

(2) 'the attorney['s] skill, experience, and reputation' and

(3) 'the prevailing market rates in the relevant community.' *Covington*, 57 F.3d at 1107.

Of these three sub-elements, the District contests only the prevailing market rate in the relevant community."

In DC federal courts, a "matrix" to determine fees is often used based on the *Laffey* cases in the early '80's. One such "*Laffey Matrix*" is inflation based and the United States Attorney's Office (USAO) maintains and updates that matrix. The other matrix relies on "legal-services inflation" (LSI).

"During Eley's IDEA litigation, the USAO *Laffey Matrix* suggests that a litigator specializing in complex federal litigation with 11 to 19 years' experience should receive between $420 and $445 per hour . . . [and] the LSI *Laffey Matrix* suggests that a litigator specializing in complex federal litigation with 11 to 19 years' experience should receive $625 per hour."

The district court judge referred the attorney fee request to a magistrate who concluded that "the *Laffey Matrix* was created for 'complex federal litigation in the District of Columbia' and it contains presumptive maximum rates, id. at 9 (emphasis added), the magistrate found the maximum *Laffey* rates 'not appropriate' for Eley's IDEA litigation, id. at 10. Multiplying the number of hours by his chosen hourly rate, the magistrate recommended that Eley receive $40,620.32 in fees and costs."

"Both sides objected to the magistrate's report and recommendation. Eley challenged the magistrate's choice of prevailing market rate, and the District attacked on multiple fronts, urging the district court to reduce the award from $40,620.32 to no more than $2,900.62. The district court largely ruled in favor of Eley. The court first compared the USAO and LSI *Laffey Matrices*, ultimately deciding to use the LSI *Laffey Matrix*."

The district court "concluded that Eley's lawyer's verified statement, 'as well as [Kavanaugh's] declaration explaining the methodology and rationale for the updated rates,' demonstrated that the LSI *Laffey Matrix* was 'an appropriate measure of the prevailing community rates for attorneys in the Washington, D.C. area.'"

The court of appeals questioned both the use of the LSI *Laffey Matrix* and her supporting documentation. "As noted, Eley had the burden 'to produce satisfactory evidence—in addition to [her] attorney's own affidavits—that [her] requested rates are in line with those prevailing in the community for similar services by lawyers of reasonably comparable skill, experience, and reputation.'"

"Eley directed the district court to only four cases that had employed the LSI *Laffey Matrix*—none of which was an IDEA case. The District, on the other hand, cited more than forty IDEA cases in which IDEA plaintiffs had received attorneys' fees awards based on prevailing hourly rates at least $180 lower than the $625 rate applied by the district court here. On this record, Eley has not met her burden of justifying the reasonableness of the rates."

"We conclude that, in relieving Eley of her burden, the district court abused its discretion . . . [and] vacate the district court's fee award and remand for proceedings consistent with this opinion."

Leggett v. DC Pub. Sch.
793 F.3d 59 (DC Cir. 2015)
July 10, 2015

In this DC tuition reimbursement case, the court of appeals relied heavily upon my case, *Florence County Sch. Dist. IV v. Carter*, 501 U.S. 7 (1993), and used many quotes from the decision by Supreme Court that ruled 9-0 in our favor.

The hearing officer and district court judge found that DCPS failed to offer FAPE and yet the parent, Jane Leggett, was unable to recover tuition because the private school was a boarding school, not a day school. The parent tried to enroll her daughter in a private day school but was not successful.

Jane Leggett was represented by counsel at the due process hearing and before the district court. However, after losing at both levels, and having to pay ongoing tuition ($58,000/year) for her daughter, and presumably indebted to her counsel, she represented herself, pro se, before the court of appeals.

Judge Tatel opened the decision with this statement: "This case presents a recurring issue under the Individuals with Disabilities Education Act: When a parent chooses, without school officials' consent, to send her child to a private school, under what circumstances must the school district reimburse the parent for the costs of attending that school? Here, the parent chose a private boarding school, and both a hearing officer and the district court denied reimbursement because, in their view, the child had no need to be in a residential program."

In a nutshell, the parent lost at the due process hearing and at the district court because the private school placement was a boarding school, not a private day school.

"In this case, we must determine the precise contours of these requirements: Under what circumstances does the school district's failure to offer an IEP by the start of the year—either in a public or private school—amount to a denial of FAPE? When is a private boarding-school placement 'proper under the Act'? And what factors must a court consider when addressing the equities?"

As background, K.E. attended DC Public Schools from Kindergarten to her eleventh grade. She received special education services in elementary school for her learning disabilities, but not at middle or high school. Upon entering Wilson High School in 2009, Jane Leggett asked that her daughter be evaluated for her learning disabilities. The court noted, "The school agreed to perform that evaluation, but it had failed to do so by the fall of 2011 when K.E. began her junior year."

"By October of that year, although K.E. had been identified as a student of above-average intelligence, she was failing most of her classes, often due to inattention, disorganization, and anxiety."

A few months later, in February 2012, "Leggett again asked school officials to evaluate her daughter. When the school district refused—instead recommending that Leggett pay for a private assessment—Leggett filed a due process complaint seeking a comprehensive evaluation to determine K.E.'s eligibility for special education . . . When school officials finally agreed to undertake the necessary testing, Leggett withdrew her complaint."

Subsequent evaluations recommended that K.E. "be placed in a 'small, highly structured therapeutic classroom with a low student to teacher ratio throughout her day' and proposed a 'more intensive educational program' for K.E., including benchmarking of reading fluency, strategies to support reading comprehension, and evidence-based cognitive behavioral strategies for depression and anxiety."

Since the 2011-2012 school year was ending, Wilson High held two IEP meetings in June but failed to complete the IEP. They agreed to meet in August to finalize the IEP.

"The team also recommended that, in the meantime, K.E. receive counseling over the summer. On June 21, just a week after the IEP team had met, Leggett emailed Wilson's Special Education Coordinator to pin down the details of the August meeting and to ask for guidance on the recommended summer counseling. She received no response. Facing a summer without the recommended assistance, Leggett next left a voicemail message for the Coordinator. No response. Finally, Leggett sent a letter in early July to the same effect. Again, nothing."

"Having received no indication that DCPS would finalize K.E.'s IEP before the school year began, and thus with no assurance that K.E. would get the special-education services she needed, Leggett began exploring alternative placements. She investigated 'literally dozens' of possible schools, but she found only two that appeared to meet K.E.'s needs. One, a local private day school, rejected K.E. on the ground that a 'highly structured, supportive school or therapeutic setting' would better serve her needs. The other, the Grier School—a boarding school in Pennsylvania—accepted her for the upcoming term."

"On August 6, just three weeks before the Wilson school year would begin, Leggett sent DCPS written notice, as the Act requires, see 20 U.S.C. §1412(10)(C)(iii)(I)(bb), that she would be withdrawing K.E. from Wilson and seeking public funding for her placement at the Grier School.

Critical for our purposes, Leggett's communication made clear that she 'remain[ed] open to' the possibility that K.E. could return to Wilson if the school offered her a satisfactory IEP . . . Again, no response. Having heard nothing by August 17, just 10 days before the first day of the Wilson school year, Leggett filed a new due-process complaint seeking either an acceptable IEP at Wilson or reimbursement for the cost of attending Grier."

"Five days before the first day of school, Leggett finally heard from DCPS when school officials contacted her to schedule a "resolution meeting." The record does not indicate what happened at that meeting, and although the parties agreed at oral argument that the meeting occurred on August 29, neither could offer any details. Everyone agrees, however, that the session resulted in no IEP. On September 4, without an IEP in place and with no guarantee that K.E. would receive the special education she required if she returned to Wilson, Leggett enrolled her at Grier."

"Meanwhile, on September 11, more than two weeks into the Wilson school year, K.E.'s IEP team met once again to try to finalize her plan. By September 24, officials had come up with a document, but according to Leggett, the IEP was riddled with errors and failed to include many of the special-education programs K.E. needed."

"In late October, a Hearing Officer took up Leggett's request for reimbursement for the tuition and fees she had paid to Grier. Although the Officer found that DCPS had denied K.E. a free appropriate public education, he nonetheless concluded that the Grier placement was improper because K.E. had no need to be in a residential program. See Hearing Officer Determination at 16–20. Accordingly, he denied Leggett any reimbursement at all."

Leggett appealed to the district court, which, on a motion for summary judgment, upheld the determination of the Hearing Officer.

On appeal, the circuit court addressed whether the failure by DCPS was a procedural violation or did it affect the student's substantive right to an appropriate education, the remedies being different. DCPS argued, "it was Leggett who transformed the absence of an IEP from a procedural deficiency into a substantive harm."

The court responded, "Here Leggett had made K.E. available for evaluation, and she remained open to leaving her daughter at Wilson until she had to enroll at Grier. DCPS had until the beginning of the Wilson school year to create an IEP for K.E. It is entirely illogical for the school system to blame Leggett for its failure to do so."

"[I]t was DCPS's failure to develop an IEP that forced Leggett's hand. School officials acknowledged in June 2012 that K.E. needed an IEP. Yet they responded to none of Leggett's communications, fulfilled none of their statutory responsibilities, and left her in a position in which the only way to find out if DCPS would ever develop an IEP would have been to leave K.E. at Wilson, despite lacking any evidence that the school was close to having a plan ready. IDEA prohibits school districts from forcing parents to make that kind of decision."

"For all of these reasons, we agree with the Hearing Officer and the district court that DCPS denied K.E. a free appropriate public education by failing to have an IEP in place by the beginning of the school year."

"Because Grier was 'necessary' to K.E.'s education and because it was 'reasonably calculated to provide educational benefit, it was 'proper under the Act.' Under the statute and regulations, therefore, DCPS must reimburse Leggett for her costs. Although this conclusion applies most comfortably to Grier's tuition, it extends to room and board as well. The regulation expressly requires that 'the placement, including . . . room and board, shall be provided at no cost to the [child] or his or her parents or guardian' if it is "necessary" to the child's education. 34 C.F.R. §104.33(c)(3). Because K.E. could not possibly have attended Grier, some three hours from the District, without living there, the school's residential program was clearly 'necessary' and thus reimbursable."

The court then concluded the comprehensive decision by addressing the argument raised in so many special education cases—that a ruling in the parent's favor will bankrupt the school district:

"We understand that requiring a school system to reimburse parents for the costs of expensive private boarding schools diverts funds away from public education. But where, as here, the school district has failed to provide a free appropriate public education in either a public or a non-residential private school, where the residential school the parent selected is 'reasonably calculated to provide educational benefits,' where the residential component of that school is 'necessary' for the child to attend that school, and where the school system has not shown that the parent acted unreasonably, IDEA requires reimbursement for tuition, room and board, and other related educational expenses—even if costly. Moreover, and contrary to the district court's fear that if Leggett prevails parents will have 'carte blanche' to choose an expensive private school, the Supreme Court emphasized in *Carter* that under IDEA, school officials have complete control over the situation, i.e., to avoid burdensome reimbursement obligations, they need only offer each child a free appropriate public education, either in a public school or in a private school the district chooses. *Carter*, 510 U.S. at 15–16. This, according to the Court, 'is IDEA's mandate, and school officials who conform to it need not worry about reimbursement claims.' Id. at 15. Like any other public school system, then, DCPS can avoid cases like this one simply by ensuring that its employees understand and fulfill the school system's obligations under IDEA—to provide a FAPE and to do so in a timely manner—and that they answer the phone when it rings."

"For the foregoing reasons, we reverse and remand for further proceedings consistent with this opinion."

McAllister v. DC Pub. Sch.
794 F.3d 15 (DC Cir. 2015)
July 14, 2015

This case is based on the decision in *Arlington Central Sch. Dist. v. Murphy*, 548 U.S. 291 (2006) where the Supreme Court held that prevailing parents cannot be reimbursed for their expert witness fees, only for attorneys' fees. The "expert" in the *Murphy* case was Marilyn Arons, a lay advocate who represented the parents at the due process hearing and later testified as an "expert." At the conclusion of the *Murphy* case, the parents' attorney sought fees for all her work. Marilyn Arons was not an employee of the law firm that represented the Murphy family in federal court.

In *McAllister*, Sharon Millis is a lay advocate who is employee of the law firm. She testified as an expert witness in the case. The court explained:

"Plaintiffs in these consolidated cases—parents of children with special needs in the District of Columbia Public Schools (DCPS)—brought suit against the school system, alleging various IDEA violations. After prevailing on all claims, plaintiffs sought some $386,000 in attorneys' fees for work performed by their law firm, Tyrka & Associates. The district court disallowed more than fifty percent of the requested fees, including $23,757 for work performed by Sharon Millis, whom Tyrka identified as a paralegal. The district court, relying on Millis's own description of her professional role, as well as its finding in a prior case classifying Millis as an expert, concluded that Millis had performed as an expert, not a paralegal, and that fees for her work were therefore non-recoverable as part of 'reasonable attorneys' fees.' The court ultimately awarded plaintiffs $159,133 in attorneys' fees."

"Plaintiffs now appeal, challenging only the district court's denial of fees for Sharon Millis's work."

This case relates to the differences between a paralegal and a lay advocate and whether the fees incurred by the lay advocate are reimbursable as attorney's fees or are barred under the U.S. Supreme Court's *Murphy* prohibition on payment of fees for experts. Is the lay advocate a paralegal or is the lay advocate an expert?

"[P]laintiffs contend [that] Millis's work is compensable under *Jenkins* because her 'professional role . . . perfectly meets the ABA definition of a paralegal/legal assistant' as 'a person, qualified by education, training or work experience who is employed or retained by a lawyer . . . who performs specifically delegated substantive legal work for which a lawyer is responsible.'"

"To be sure, paralegal costs may be recoverable under IDEA. After all, given that the Court announced its holding in *Jenkins*—that section 1988 'clearly' authorizes recovery of fees for paralegals—before Congress enacted IDEA, and given that IDEA uses the same language as section 1988, public officials signing up for IDEA funds were on notice that prevailing plaintiffs could recover paralegal costs. But we need not definitively resolve that question because even if the ABA standard is the controlling definition of 'paralegal,' plaintiffs have failed to show that the district court abused its discretion in concluding that Sharon Millis did not perform 'substantive legal work.'"

"To begin with, in her own résumé, Millis describes herself as an 'Independent Special Education Advocate/Expert for Special Education Attorneys/Courts/Parents,' and lists 'core competencies' in, among other things, expert testimony regarding special education, special education curriculum development, and analysis of therapeutic models for special needs students. Nowhere does the résumé say anything about legal training or paralegal experience."

"The affidavit submitted by firm founder Douglas Tyrka is consistent with Millis's résumé. Although Tyrka describes every other firm employee as 'a fully trained paralegal' trained by 'paralegals and attorneys of the firm,' he calls Millis a special education professional with forty years of experience. To be sure, the affidavit also says that Millis 'performed all of her work under the supervision of the firm's attorneys' and that she 'trained [Tyrka] in the practice of special education law in the District of Columbia.' But neither of these statements

demonstrates that Millis herself actually engaged in the kind of substantive legal work normally undertaken by paralegals."

"Equally significant, the billing records reflect a dramatic difference between Millis's work and that of the 'fully trained paralegals.' The paralegals all engaged in traditional paralegal activities, e.g., making phone calls, maintaining files, and preparing correspondence, whereas Millis's work involved substantive special education tasks, e.g., reviewing neuropsychological and auditory processing reports, participating in multidisciplinary team meetings, and testifying at due process hearings. Tyrka & Associates Billing Records 1-73.

"All of this—Millis's résumé, Tyrka's affidavit, and the billing records—demonstrates that the district court did not abuse its discretion in concluding that Millis is what she says she is: a highly experienced special education consultant and expert."

"Second, plaintiffs argue that Millis's work is compensable because '[u]nlike the *Murphy* plaintiffs, [they] did not retain Ms. Millis separately,' but instead she 'was employed by [a law firm], where she worked directly under lawyer supervision.' Again, plaintiffs ignore what *Murphy* requires: Whether independently employed by plaintiffs (*Murphy*) or hired by a law firm (this case), plaintiffs must demonstrate that 'IDEA gives [states] unambiguous notice regarding liability for expert fees.' *Murphy*, 548 U.S. at 301. Neither in the district court nor here have plaintiffs even attempted to satisfy that requirement."

"For the foregoing reasons, we affirm the judgment of the district court."

MO v. NYC Dept. Ed.
793 F.3d 236 (2nd Cir. 2015)
July 15, 2015

This is a tuition reimbursement case in which the parents lost at due process, lost at the review level, lost at the district court, appealed to the second circuit, and lost again.

The parents unilaterally placed their child into a private day special education school and sued for reimbursement. They based their rejection of the public school placement on their perception that the IEP could not be implemented at that school.

"By Final Notice of Recommendation dated July 6, 2011, the DOE informed M.O. and G.O. that D.O. had been reassigned to P.S. 159 for the 2011-2012 school year. M.O. responded, in a July 11, 2011 letter, that she had called P.S. 159 but was unable to visit because the school was not in session during the summer months. The July 11, 2011 letter further advised that M.O. and G.O. could not accept D.O.'s placement at P.S. 159 because they had no idea whether the school was appropriate and that they would send D.O. to the Lowell School and seek tuition reimbursement if an appropriate placement was not offered in a timely manner. In August 2011, M.O. and G.O. informed the DOE of their decision to enroll D.O. in the Lowell School for the 2011-2012 school year based on their belief that D.O. was not offered an appropriate placement. D.O. attended third grade at the Lowell School for the 2011-2012 school year."

"In September 2011, M.O. and G.O. initiated their reimbursement action for D.O.'s unilateral placement in the Lowell School by filing a due process complaint and request for a hearing before an IHO. The due process complaint alleged that D.O.'s IEP was substantively inadequate for the following reasons: (1) the size of the proposed classroom, the student-teacher ratio, and the size of the school building were inappropriate; (2) the level of related services mandated by the IEP was inappropriate; (3) the IEP's recommendation that D.O. repeat the second grade was detrimental; (4) the IEP failed to address D.O.'s need for a language-based pro-

gram; and (5) the IEP failed to address D.O.'s need for 1:1 reading support."

"The district court observed that, under this Court's decision in R.E., evaluation of whether a child was denied a FAPE 'must focus on the written plan offered to the parents. Speculation that the school district will not adequately adhere to the IEP is not an appropriate basis for unilateral placement.'"

In affirming the dismissal by the district court, the court of appeals explained: "Turning to the case at bar, we note that the due process complaint's challenges to P.S. 159 were not of the type permitted . . . prospective challenges to P.S. 159's capacity to provide the services mandated by the IEP. They were, instead, substantive attacks on D.O.'s IEP that were couched as challenges to the adequacy of P.S. 159. For example, the due process complaint challenged D.O.'s placement at P.S. 159 on the grounds that the school building was too large, the student-teacher ratio was too large, and the language-based program was inappropriate, which were the very same challenges directed at D.O.'s IEP. These challenges, therefore, do not relate to P.S. 159's capacity to implement the IEP; they relate to the appropriateness of the IEP's substantive recommendations. Because the substantive adequacy of the IEP must be determined by reference to the written IEP itself, the school district did not have the burden to produce evidence demonstrating P.S. 159's adequacy in response to these arguments. Similarly, although M.O. testified that she visited P.S. 159 and found that the placement was inappropriate, her assertion was based on her own belief that 'if was put in there, he would shut down completely,' rather than on P.S. 159's lack of IEP-mandated services."

"For the foregoing reasons, we affirm the judgment of the district court."

TB v. San Diego
9th Cir. – July 31, 2015

This California case is about attorney's fees and rejection of a settlement offer. The Court held that the parents' rejection was justified.

". . . the Brenneises and their attorneys sought attorneys' fees and costs for their partial victory before the ALJ. The district court awarded them approximately $50,000 for attorneys' fees, substantially less than the $1.4 million that was requested. The principal basis for denying most of the fee request was a determination by the district court that the Brenneises had unreasonably rejected a settlement offer made by the school district shortly before the start of the due process hearing."

"The IDEA provides that attorneys' fees should not be awarded if the parents do not accept a timely settlement offer, "the relief finally obtained by the parents is not more favorable to the parents than the offer of settlement," and the parents' rejection of the settlement offer was not "substantially justified." 20 U.S.C. §1415(i)(3)(D)(i)(III)

"We conclude, contrary to the district court, that the relief obtained through the ALJ's decision was more favorable to the parents than the offer of settlement and that the parents were substantially justified in rejecting the offer, so the district court's denial of fees on that basis must be set aside. For that and other reasons, we vacate the district court's determination of fees and costs and remand that matter for further consideration as well."

Sneitzer v. Iowa Dept of Ed
796 F.3d 942 (8th Cir. 2015)
August 7, 2015

In this Iowa case, the parents' request for tuition reimbursement was denied. The child has autism, is very high functioning, was raped during a summer cruise and began to display emotional problems upon return to school.

The parents eventually placed her into a private residential program and sought reimbursement. Parents lost at due process, lost at district court and the Eighth Circuit concurred.

"And, as the ALJ held, following an exhaustive review of the relevant medical, psychological, and educational witnesses, there was simply not enough evidence that K.S. was unable to return to Kennedy in August 2012, or that returning would cause her severe and lasting psychological harm, as alleged by Renee."

"Many of Renee's expert witnesses at the due process hearing who opined about such harm had not communicated with the district personnel who spent time observing K.S. at Kennedy while K.S. ... One of Renee's expert witnesses admitted that she did not know that K.S. had, in fact, spent a good number of days in the Kennedy school building over the summer months. Indeed, Renee and her witnesses spent a substantial amount of time at the August 16 IEP meeting advocating that K.S. should return to Kennedy and be placed in the Happiness show choir."

"The ALJ further found, and we agree, that each incident of bullying that was reported to the school was promptly investigated and resolved, and the district presented substantial evidence refuting the claim that K.S. was subjected to ongoing bullying or harassment."

"K.S.'s one-on-one paraprofessional who accompanied K.S. nearly every day of the 2012 spring semester testified at the due process hearing that she never witnessed K.S. being bullied by other students, nor did K.S. report to her that K.S. had been bullied."

Endrew v. Douglas Sch Dist.
798 F.3d 1329 (10ᵗʰ Cir. 2015)
August 25, 2015

In this Colorado tuition reimbursement case, the parents lost at due process and in district court. The parents argued that the data collection was insufficient, that the school failed to do an FBA and BIP, and they unsuccessfully advocated for a new definition of "educational benefit."

The parents "argue the ALJ and the district court erred in concluding the IEP was substantively adequate because (1) Drew made no measurable progress on the goals set in his past IEPs, and (2) there was no consideration of Drew's escalating behavioral problems."

"The first procedural deficiency alleged by the parents is the District's failure to adequately report Drew's progress toward the annual goals and objectives listed in his IEPs. They contend the lack of progress reporting deprived them of meaningful participation in Drew's education. We agree with the District that, even assuming a procedural violation, the District's progress reporting did not result in the denial of a FAPE."

"As an initial matter, the District concedes that the progress reporting on Drew's IEPs could have been more robust. As the ALJ found, Drew's IEPs contain little or no progress reporting or measurement data and where progress was reported, it was 'lacking in detail' or limited to 'conclusory statements about whether [Drew] was on track to meet the expectations of the plan and whether the objective had been completed or would be continued.' But the District contends what was reported was sufficient for the parents to assess Drew's progress and that whatever deficiencies existed, the parents' involvement in Drew's education did not suffer as a result."

"Drew's parents were not absentee caretakers; they were just the opposite. The ALJ found that, in addition to the progress reporting that was included on Drew's IEPs, there was substantial evidence of the parents' awareness of Drew's progress and of their active participation in his education. For instance, the ALJ found the parents were "in constant communication" with

Drew's special education teacher both through face-to-face meetings and a "back-and-forth notebook," which was used to inform the parents of what occurred at school and to inform Drew's teacher of what happened in the home."

"The parents' second procedural argument is that the District's handling of Drew's behavioral needs amounted to a substantive denial of a FAPE. Specifically, they criticize (1) the District's failure to conduct a functional behavior assessment (FBA) before implementing a behavior plan for Drew, and (2) even absent the FBA, the District's failure to put in place an appropriate behavioral intervention plan (BIP) to address Drew's increasing behavioral issues."

"They argue our opinion in *Jefferson County School District v. Elizabeth E.*, 702 F.3d 1227 (10th Cir. 2012) abandoned the 'some educational benefit' standard previously articulated in our cases (and applied by the ALJ and the district court) in favor of a heightened 'meaningful educational benefit' standard."

The Court refused to redefine *Rowley* and adopt the "meaningful" standard, noting "In our view, those citations — one to a circuit following a "meaningful educational benefit" standard and one following the "some educational benefit" standard — make it clear that the fleeting references to "meaningful educational benefit" in *Jefferson County* is nothing more than that. "

BS + KS v. Anoka Hennepin Pub Sch.
799 F.3d 1217 (8ᵗʰ Cir. 2015)
September 2, 2015

In this Minnesota case, relying upon representations of counsel about the duration of the due process hearing, the ALJ restricted parent's counsel's examination of witnesses when the attorney exceeded the allotted time.

"B.S. was, at the time of the hearing, a sixteen-year-old identified with attention deficit hyperactivity disorder and has had an individualized education program (IEP) with the district. A dispute arose between the parents and the school district over the IEP, and the parents requested a due process hearing pursuant to 20 U.S.C. § 1415 in May 2013. During a pretrial conference, B.S.'s counsel indicated that she usually needed a day and a half to present evidence, and counsel for the school district indicated one day would be sufficient. The Administrative Law Judge (ALJ) accordingly allotted nine hours of hearing time (eighteen hours total, divided evenly) for each party to present the testimony and cross-examination of its witnesses, and counsel were directed to plan their hearing presentations accordingly."

"In the middle of B.S.'s examination of this second witness, the ALJ reminded B.S.'s counsel that the nine-hour time limit set at the pretrial conference would be enforced, and offered counsel the opportunity to reorder the presentation of evidence accordingly. Counsel for B.S. objected to the enforcement of the time limits and continued on with the lengthy examination of the special-education case manager. B.S's time expired while examining the special-education case manager, and B.S. was not allowed to question witnesses further or cross-examine the district's witnesses."

"In its final order, the ALJ surmised that based upon the offer of proof, B.S. would have needed three more days of hearing to present this additional evidence."

"Although the district court considered the entirety of B.S.'s substantive claims on appeal from the ALJ, the only thing being challenged here is the propriety of the ALJ's time limits . . . Given Minnesota's statutory mandate vesting hearing officers with broad authority to manage the IDEA due process hearing, we agree with the district court that our review of this issue is for an abuse of discretion." The Court of Appeals affirmed the ruling against the parents.

DM v. NJ Dept of Ed.
801 F.3d 205 (3rd Cir. 2015)
September 10, 2015

In this New Jersey case, a child attended a private special ed school that integrated students from regular education for part of the school day. The State Dept of Ed attempted to shut the program, as structured, down.

"The Learning Center for Exceptional Children is a private school for students with disabilities. It opened in 1978. During the times relevant to this lawsuit, LCEC leased classroom space in a building in Clifton, New Jersey. Also sharing this space was a private school for regular-education students, Today's Learning Center. The principal of LCEC is also the principal of TLC."

"LCEC was specifically selected as the out-of-district educational placement for E.M. due to her unique academic and social/emotional needs."

"In December 2013, after an on-site inspection, the Department requested a "statement of assurance that nonpublic school students from TLC are not in class with public school students from LCEC.'"

"LCEC and E.M., through her parents D.M. and L.M., sued the Department. LCEC sought injunctive and declaratory relief allowing LCEC to accept new students and to educate its public-school students with TLC's regular-education students."

The District Court granted the injunction only in regard to the child pursuant to the stay put rule.

"E.M. believes that the Department's interpretation of the scope of LCEC's approvals is incorrect, arbitrary, and capricious. By imposing its interpretation of the scope of LCEC's approvals on E.M., the Department would prevent E.M. from having her IEP implemented as worded: that she attend LCEC and integrated classes with students at TLC. Because receiving an education in compliance with her IEP is a part of receiving a free appropriate public education under IDEA, see 20 U.S.C. §1401(9)(D), the Department is thus arguably interfering with her ability to receive a free appropriate public education."

The decision included a lengthy discussion about stay put, educational placement. and noted that exhaustion was not required. The Court remanded the case back to the District Court for further fact finding.

AF + Christine B. v. Espanola Pub. Sch.
801 F.3d 1245 (10ᵗʰ Cir. 2015)
September 15, 2015

After a New Mexico parent requested a due process hearing, she settled her IDEA claim at mediation. Then she filed suit in federal court for damages, pursuant to ADA and Section 504. The Court dismissed her claim because she failed to exhaust her administrative remedies under IDEA.

"This case ended almost before it began. Christine B. filed her administrative complaint, just as she had to. But before any hearing could be held, she sought to mediate her dispute. And the choice proved fruitful, for in the end the parties signed a settlement agreement. Indeed, as a result of the settlement, Christine B. asked the administrative agency to dismiss her IDEA claims with prejudice, something the agency duly did."

"But after ending her suit she sought to begin it again. Despite the satisfactory result she received through mediation, Christine B. later took to mind the thought she might sue — and she did. To be sure, her lawsuit didn't seek to press a claim under IDEA, itself a tacit acknowledgment that her mediated settlement precluded that option. Instead, she sued under the Americans with Disabilities Act, the Rehabilitation Act, and 42 U.S.C. § 1983, though the allegations in her federal court complaint and those in her original IDEA administrative complaint are nearly identical: both allege that A.F. suffers from the same disabilities and both contend that the school district failed to take her disabilities into account in her educational program . . . the district court dismissed her

lawsuit and it is this result she now asks us to overturn."

"It's clear Christine B. cannot bring an IDEA lawsuit in federal court after choosing to settle her IDEA claims and agreeing to their dismissal with prejudice . . . it follows ineluctably that an ADA or Rehabilitation Act or § 1983 lawsuit seeking the same relief is also barred."

The case was dismissed for failing to exhaust her administrative remedies. Judge Briscoe wrote a dissent that was several times longer than the opinion of the majority. He opened:

"In this case of first impression, the majority misreads 20 U.S.C. §1415(l) to require a litigant, such as plaintiff A.F., to forgo any resolution of her claim under the Individuals with Disabilities Education Act (IDEA) in order to preserve the ability to seek remedies in federal court under acts other than the IDEA. More specifically, a claimant under the IDEA must now, in order to later be able to file suit in federal court under other related statutes, refuse to settle her IDEA claim during the preliminary meeting required by 20 U.S.C. §1415(f)(1)(B) or the mediation process described in 20 U.S.C. §1415(e), and must also lose in both the due process hearing outlined in 20 U.S.C. §1415(f)(1)(A) and the subsequent administrative appeal out-lined in 20 U.S.C. §1415(g). This was clearly not the intent of Congress and, ironically enough, harms the interests of the children that IDEA was intended to protect. As a result, I respectfully dissent."

GL v. Ligonier Valley Sch Dist
802 F.3d 601 (3d Cir. 2015)
September 22, 2015

The issue in this Pennsylvania case was whether the two-year statute of limitations had a subsequent limit on the nature and duration of a compensatory education remedy. The Court held that it does not.

"We now conclude, after careful consideration of the parties' plain language arguments, the statutory context and structure, the DOE's interpretive guidance, and the legislative history, that §1415(b)(6)(B) is simply an inartful attempt to mirror §1415(f)(3)(C)'s two-year statute of limitations. That is, both sections reflect the same two-year filing deadline for a due process complaint after the reasonable discovery of an injury, and §1415(b)(6)(B) neither imposes a pleading requirement nor in any respect alters the courts' broad power under the IDEA to provide a complete remedy for the violation of a child's right to a free appropriate public education."

"For these reasons, we hold today that, absent one of the two statutory exceptions found in §1415(f)(3)(D), parents have two years from the date they knew or should have known of the violation to request a due process hearing through the filing of an administrative complaint and that, assuming parents timely file that complaint and liability is proven, Congress did not abrogate our longstanding precedent that "a disabled child is entitled to compensatory education for a period equal to the period of deprivation, but excluding the time reasonably required for the school district to rectify the problem."

The Court explained that the compensatory education remedy may be for longer than two years, i.e., "when a school district has failed in that responsibility and parents have taken appropriate and timely action under the IDEA, then that child is entitled to be made whole with nothing less than a 'complete' remedy. Compensatory education is crucial to achieve that goal, and the courts, in the exercise of their broad discretion, may award it to whatever extent necessary to make up for the child's lost progress and to restore the child to the educational path he or she would have traveled but for the deprivation."

OS v. Fairfax County Sch. Bd.
804 F.3d 354 (4th Cir. 2015)
October 19, 2015

In this Virginia case, the parents objected to the school's IEP and sought a one-to-one aide and Extended School Year (ESY). Failing that, the parents requested a due process hearing in an unsuccessful attempt to persuade the conservative Fourth Circuit to abandon the *Rowley* standard and create a new definition of "educational benefit."

At the due process hearing, the only witnesses called by the parents were themselves. After the parents lost at due process and in district court, they appealed to the court of appeals.

"After conducting a three-day hearing, in which the hearing officer heard from fourteen witnesses and received over 200 exhibits, the officer issued a detailed written opinion. In that opinion, the officer first recognized that the IEP team had complied with the IDEA's procedural requirements in developing O.S.'s IEPs, and then evaluated the implementation of the IEPs. The officer considered O.S.'s IEPs and progress reports particularly important exhibits and noted that all of the testifying witnesses were 'open and honest.'"

"The officer then credited ten witnesses in particular, who were O.S.'s teachers and other educational experts. All testified to O.S.'s progress during kindergarten and first grade, and explained why each additional accommodation that his parents requested was unnecessary for second grade. While acknowledging that the IDEA does not require parents to present expert testimony, the officer noted that, in contrast to the School Board's showing, O.S.'s parents 'offer[ed] virtually no witnesses, other than the parent,' to support their position. The hearing officer concluded that the School Board had provided O.S. a FAPE."

"Initially and principally, O.S. argues that the district court applied the wrong standard in evaluating whether he received a FAPE. Specifically, he maintains that in the current version of the IDEA, a FAPE requires 'meaningful' rather than 'some' educational benefit."

"O.S. asks us to find that, in the 1997 and 2004 amendments to the statute, Congress replaced the *Rowley* standard. He points to the 2004 congressional findings in the IDEA preamble as evidence that the law now focuses on results rather than mere access. The congressional findings lament 'low expectations' of children with disabilities, and state that educating children with disabilities is 'more effective' when there are 'high expectations' of them 'to the maximum extent possible.'" See 20 U.S.C. §1400(c) (2012). While the EHA succeeded in providing access to education and improving educational results, *id.*, O.S. argues that the IDEA aimed to go further."

"For our part, we are loath to hold, without any express acknowledgment of its intent to do so, that Congress abrogated Supreme Court precedent. We note that recently the Tenth Circuit also rejected a similar contention that a heightened 'meaningful benefit' standard had replaced the 'some benefit' standard. *Endrew F. ex rel. Joseph F. v. Douglas Cty. Sch. Dist. RE-1*, 798 F.3d 1329, 1338-41 (10th Cir. 2015)."

"In this circuit, the standard remains the same as it has been for decades: a school provides a FAPE so long as a child receives some educational benefit, meaning a benefit that is more than minimal or trivial, from special instruction and services."

('IDEA'). J.F., a fourteen-year-old boy with learning disabilities, relocated with his family from New Jersey's Westwood Regional School District ('Westwood') to the Byram Township School District ('Byram'). He contends on appeal that the stay-put provision requires Byram to pay for him to remain at a private school outside of Byram during the pendency of a due process petition that he is pressing. We disagree. Byram's obligation under the IDEA is to provide J.F. with services comparable to what he received from Westwood until it either implements the program designed for J.F. by Westwood or designs its own program. The District Court concluded that Byram has met its obligation, and we will affirm."

"Although the 'stay-put' provision is meant to preserve the status quo, we recognize that when a student transfers educational jurisdictions, the status quo no longer exists."

"The question remains whether Byram has met its obligation under §1414(d)(2)(C)(i)(I). The ALJ and the District Court both found that Byram offered services comparable to those provided for in the Westwood IEP."

The Court held that the new school district was not required to pay for a private placement that was funded by the former school district.

JF v. Byram Township Bd of Ed
3rd Cir. – October 29, 2015

In this New Jersey case, the child was enrolled in a private special education school with tuition paid for by the school district. When the family moved to a new school district, pursuant to the "stay put" and "comparable IEP" statutes, the parents requested that the new district continue to pay their child's tuition at the private school. The district declined.

"This appeal presents a question about the scope of the 'stay-put' provision of the Individuals with Disabilities Education Act

Phyllene v. Huntsville City Sch Bd.
11th Cir. – October 30, 2015

Phyllene v. Huntsville City Sch Bd "When M.W. was twenty-one months old, she underwent the first of many surgeries to place tympanostomy tubes in her ears . . . by the time M.W. was sixteen years old, she had undergone seven surgeries to place or replace the tubes in her ears."

From Kindergarten until she was withdrawn from public school in the 10th grade, M.W. also had significant learning problems in reading and math, organizational problems, and test problems.

In second grade, her teacher recommended that she be evaluated to determine if she had a disability and needed special education services. The evaluation found that her IQ was within the average range but she was performing below grade level in reading and math.

As MW prepared to enter 10th grade, her reading was at the 3.6 grade level while math was at the 2.6 grade level . . . However, the school did not evaluate MW's hearing to determine if her hearing loss was affecting her learning and academic progress. "

When M.W. prepared to transfer to a private school in tenth grade, her mother had her evaluated and also filed a request for a due process hearing.

"...These evaluations found "a longstanding, fluctuating conductive hearing loss that caused M.W. to have moderate to severe difficulty understanding speech . . . [her] hearing was so poor, she spent most of her energy trying to hear what was being said."

"Aside from the requirements with respect to reevaluations, the IDEA provides that '[e]ach local educational agency shall ensure that . . . the child is assessed in all areas of suspected disability.'

"... a statement that a student's hearing is 'worse' than it was two years ago may not, in and of itself, prompt a school board to suspect a hearing impairment . . . Phyllene W. was actively seeking treatment for M.W.'s hearing loss supports a finding that the Board should have at least 'suspected' that a hearing impairment might be present."

" . . . the 2008 comment — that M.W. had a 'history of having tubes in her ears and her hearing in her left ear is worse than it was two years ago' — is evidence that further supports that the Board was on notice of the need to reevaluate M.W . . . Because the 2008 conversation regarding M.W.'s hearing loss constitutes relevant evidence, it should have been considered by the Hearing Officer.

"We find that both of these pieces of evidence — particularly when viewed against M.W.'s myriad

of other problems in school — put the Board on notice that M.W. suffered from a hearing disability that warranted further investigation . . . Phyllene W. did not request an evaluation of her daughter's hearing, the fact that she did not do so did not absolve the Board of its independent responsibility to evaluate a student suspected of a disability, regardless of whether the parent seeks an evaluation.

"While it is true . . . that Board witnesses testified that they had 'no information to create a suspicion that [M.W.] had a hearing disability that necessitated special education and related services, nor did the IEP team have any indication that a hearing evaluation was needed,' the objective record flatly contradicts the Board's witnesses . . . For this reason, the Board's contention that it did not have 'any indication that a hearing evaluation was needed' was objectively wrong, especially when coupled with the knowledge that M.W. lacked adequate abilities to demonstrate communication skills."

"Ultimately, we find that that the Board was aware that M.W. had undergone seven ear surgeries, had hearing that was worsening in her left ear to the point that treatment was necessary, and was later being fitted for a hearing aid . . . the Board should have at least 'suspected' that M.W. had a hearing impairment. It was, therefore under a duty to assess this area of suspected disability . . . the Board failed to evaluate M.W.'s hearing, and it does not appear that the Board even bothered to follow up on any hearing tests performed by M.W.'s own doctors.

"We conclude that the Board violated the procedural requirements of the IDEA by failing to evaluate M.W. when faced with evidence that she suffered from a suspected hearing impairment . . . As a result of its failure to obtain necessary medical information regarding M.W.'s hearing, the Board further failed to provide her with a FAPE. The lack of medical information rendered the accomplishment of the IDEA's goals impossible because no meaningful IEP was developed, and the IEPs put into place lacked necessary elements with respect to the services that M.W. should have been provided. In short, the Board's failure to evaluate M.W.

with respect to her hearing loss deprived M.W. of the opportunity to benefit educationally from an appropriate IEP."

"As a result of its failure to obtain necessary medical information regarding M.W.'s hearing, the Board further failed to provide her with a FAPE. The lack of medical information rendered the accomplishment of the IDEA's goals impossible because no meaningful IEP was developed, and the IEPs put into place lacked necessary elements with respect to the services that M.W. should have been provided. In short, the Board's failure to evaluate M.W. with respect to her hearing loss deprived M.W. of the opportunity to benefit educationally from an appropriate IEP."

"For the reasons discussed above, we reverse the judgment of the district court in favor of the Board and against Phyllene W. This matter is remanded to the district court for entry of judgment in favor of Appellant. We leave it to the district court to determine the precise relief to be given to Appellant."

D. G. v. New Caney Ind. Sch. Dist.
806 F.3d 310 (5th Cir. 2015)
November 10, 2015

In this case, after a parent prevailed in a due process hearing, her attorney filed for attorneys' fees.

The district court held that the attorney waited too long to file and dismissed the fee request. Noting that the statute of limitations is based on state law, not federal law, the Court of Appeals reversed.

"In this case, a mother proved in an administrative hearing that a school district had violated her child's right to a free appropriate public education by repeatedly placing him in isolation during school hours. Congress has provided that the prevailing party in such a hearing may file an action in federal court to recover reasonable attorneys' fees. This appeal asks us to decide how quickly that action must

be filed. For the reasons that follow, we REVERSE the district court's determination that a party who prevails in an administrative hearing under the Individuals with Disabilities Education Act (the 'IDEA' or 'Act') must seek attorneys' fees no later than ninety days after the hearing officer's decision."

"In addition to encouraging the filing of protective complaints in an already-overburdened court system, running a short limitations period from the time of the hearing officer's decision would leave little time for parents and school districts to agree on attorneys' fees and costs without resorting to litigation. That would contravene Congress's intent that IDEA fees and costs will '[u]sually . . . be agreed to by the public agency,' and that parents will only sue for when 'no agreement is possible.'"

"The district court erred in applying §1415(i)(2)(B)'s limitations period to this action for attorneys' fees under the IDEA by a party that prevailed at the administrative level. Because the statute contains no limitations period for such actions, the district court should have borrowed one from state law. We need not — and therefore do not — determine which period applies, an issue on which courts have splintered and congressional action would be welcome. But we do hold that the limitations period for such an action does not begin to run until the time for seeking judicial review of the underlying administrative decision passes, and that D.G.'s action was timely under any limitations period that could be borrowed. Accordingly, we REVERSE the district court's grant of summary judgment and REMAND for the district court to adjudicate the merits of D.G.'s action for attorneys' fees."

Carroll v. Lawton Indep. Sch. Dist.
805 F.3d 1222 (10ᵗʰ Cir. 2015)
November 10, 2015

In this Oklahoma case, a special education teacher abused a child with autism. Her parents filed a suit for damages under ADA and Section 504. The Court dismissed the parents' case because they did not first request a special education due process hearing, i.e., they failed to exhaust their administrative remedies.

The Court opened the decision with "This appeal arises from allegations that AKC, a child with autism, suffered abuse at school by her special-education teacher, Vickie Cantrell. AKC's parents, Ted and Bella Carroll, filed suit in federal district court against Ms. Cantrell, the school district, and others, seeking damages under the Americans with Disabilities Act (the ADA), Section 504 of the Rehabilitation Act, 42 U.S.C. § 1983, and a variety of state-law theories. The district court dismissed the Carrolls' federal claims, concluding the Carrolls had not exhausted their administrative remedies before filing suit as required by section 1415(l) of the Individuals with Disabilities Education Act (the IDEA). The district court then dismissed the Carrolls' complaint, declining to exercise supplemental jurisdiction over their state-law claims. The Carrolls appeal."

"The single issue on appeal is whether the district court erred in determining the Carrolls' federal claims were subject to the IDEA's exhaustion requirement. Because we conclude the Carrolls' complaint alleges educational injuries that could be redressed to some degree by the IDEA's administrative remedies, we agree with the district court that exhaustion of those remedies was required before the Carrolls could file suit. We therefore affirm the district court's dismissal of the Carrolls' complaint."

"The complaint alleges that Ms. Cantrell, AKC's teacher, 'punished' AKC by pulling her undergarments so hard into a 'wedgie' that AKC's underwear was torn and that 'in addition to the 'wedgie' punishment AKC had been placed in a dark closet on previous occasions." The complaint further alleges that, as a result of these 'punishments,' AKC 'suffered and continues to suffer,' particularly with respect to her education: AKC now refuses to get out of the car to go into the school building and becomes upset and agitated as she enters the school. The punishments 'damaged AKC's overall academic progress as well as her mental and emotional

health' and '[t]he impact of these punishments, coupled with AKC's autism, significantly altered AKC and her ability to attend and participate in the educational process.'"

"The Carrolls argue they are excepted or excused from the exhaustion requirement under the facts of this case. Exhaustion under the IDEA is not required 'when administrative remedies would be futile, when they would fail to provide relief, or when an agency has adopted a policy or pursued a practice of general applicability that is contrary to the law.'"

"In summary, the Carrolls have alleged that AKC's educational progress has been impeded, that she has been excluded from access to educational programs, and that she will require remedial education in the form of tutoring to return to her proper academic level. Under the IDEA, the school is entitled to 'at least the first crack at formulating a plan to overcome the consequences of educational shortfalls.' *Id.* Thus, the Carrolls were required to exhaust their administrative remedies before bringing their claims in the district court. The district court therefore properly dismissed the Carrolls' federal claims seeking relief 'also available' under the IDEA."

"The Carrolls' federal claims are therefore subject to the IDEA's exhaustion requirement."

QW v. Bd. Ed of Fayette County
6th Cir. – November 17, 2015

In this case from Kentucky, the court concluded that a child's autism did not "adversely affect" the child's "educational performance" so the child was not eligible for an IEP.

"Q.W., a high-functioning autistic student in elementary school, through his Parents, appeals the district court's judgment affirming an administrative decision finding him ineligible for special education and related services under the Individuals with Disabilities Education Act ("Act"), 20 U.S.C. §1400 et seq. The administrative board concluded that Q.W. was not statutorily disabled because his autism did not 'adversely affect [his] educational performance.' 34 C.F.R. §300.8(c)(1)(i). The district court agreed, noting that although the Act left 'educational performance' undefined, its ordinary meaning suggests 'school-based evaluation.' On appeal, the Parents argue that 'educational performance' includes not only academics but also social and psychological performance across all settings. For the following reasons, we affirm the district court's judgment."

"The Parents say that 'educational performance' includes a student's academic, social, and psychological needs. The Board agrees. Where they disagree is in the meaning of that term. The Parents' focus on Q.W.'s problematic behavior at home, while the Board focuses on the psychological and social aspects of Q.W.'s makeup that affect his school performance."

IR v. Los Angeles
805 F.3d 1164 (9th Cir. 2015)
November 17, 2015

In California, a parent consented to a portion of an IEP but not to all proposed services. If an IEP issue remains unresolved, a unique statute in California requires the school district to request a due process hearing against the child's parent. In this case, the district failed to take that step. The Court of Appeals held that this failure resulted in a denial of FAPE for the child.

The Court explained, "California Education Code §56346(f) requires school districts to initiate a due process hearing if the school district determines that a portion of an Individualized Education Program ('IEP') to which a parent does not consent is necessary to provide a child with a Free Appropriate Public Education ('FAPE') under the Individuals with Disabilities Education Act ('IDEA'). 20 U.S.C. §§1400-1450. This appeal raises the issue of a school district's responsibility to initiate a due process hearing within a reasonable time after a child's parents fail to consent to the provision of services necessary to provide a FAPE. Because we

conclude that a period of a year and a half is too long for a school district to wait to initiate a due process hearing pursuant to California Education Code § 56346(f), we reverse and remand."

"LAUSD conceded at oral argument that a school district is required to initiate a due process hearing pursuant to California Education Code § 56346(f). LAUSD argues, however, that its obligation to initiate a due process hearing was not yet triggered."

"In effect, §56346(f) compels a school district to initiate a due process hearing when the school district and the parents reach an impasse. As the goal of the statute is to ensure that the conflict between the school district and the parents is resolved promptly so that necessary components of the IEP are implemented as soon as possible, a school district may not artificially prolong the process by failing to make the necessary determination to trigger §56346(f)'s mandate."

"A school district's failure to comply with a procedural requirement, such as the requirement of California Education Code §56346(f), denies a child a FAPE when the procedural inadequacy 'result[s] in the loss of educational opportunity' or 'cause[s] a deprivation of educational benefits.' *M.M.*, 767 F.3d at 852 (quoting *N.B. v. Hellgate Elementary Sch. Dist.*, 541 F.3d 1202, 1207 (9th Cir. 2008). LAUSD's failure to comply with its obligation to initiate the adjudication process left I.R. to remain in a placement that LAUSD itself acknowledged was inappropriate. To the extent that I.R. lost an educational opportunity and was deprived of educational benefits for an unreasonably prolonged period, LAUSD can be held responsible for denying her a FAPE for that unreasonably prolonged period."

"LAUSD's failure to initiate a due process hearing, as was required under California law, directly resulted in a clear injury, namely I.R. remaining in an inappropriate program for a much longer period of time than should have been the case."

DAB v. NYC Bd. Ed.
2nd Cir. – November 18, 2015

In this tuition reimbursement case from New York, the hearing officer issued a favorable ruling but the state review officer (SRO) issued an adverse ruling. Relying on an earlier decision in *M.H. v. New York City*, the court deferred to the SRO's findings and concluded that the IEP provided an appropriate education. The court reviewed the IEP for procedural and substantive adequacy:

"After an independent review of the administrative record, we reach the same conclusion as the district court: D.B.'s IEP was sufficiently tailored to his needs to ensure meaningful progress."

The higher student teacher ratio in public school program was enhanced by a full-time behavior management paraprofessional and at least 10 hours of 1:1 related services/week. One-to-one services in private program were optimal to maximize child's potential but exceeded the requirements of IDEA. Deference to SRO was appropriate. Upheld dismissal of Section 504 claims that DOE discriminated against child because he was not vaccinated."

MS v. Marple Newtown Sch Dist.
3rd Cir. – December 22, 2105

In this case, the child had a 504 Plan, did not have an IEP, and did not receive special education services under IDEA.

After the child was repeatedly bullied and harassed and the school failed to protect her, her parent sued the school district for monetary damages under Section 504 and ADA.

The Court held that the parents should have requested a special education due process hearing because the child may have been found eligible under IDEA and may have received a remedy of educational benefit.

"According to the Complaint in this action, minor child M.S.'s sister was sexually assaulted by B.C., a boy from M.S.'s high school. Over the course of three years, and despite repeated requests to the contrary, the high school placed M.S. in classes with B.C. and his brother J.C., both of whom subjected M.S. to verbal and psychological harassment. While in high school, M.S. was diagnosed with anxiety disorder and post-traumatic stress syndrome. The school nonetheless refused to assign M.S. and her harassers to different classrooms, and M.S. eventually transferred to homebound instruction to avoid contact with the brothers."

"M.S. and her family (Appellants here) brought claims against the school district and its board (collectively, the "School District") under Section 504 of the Rehabilitation Act of 1973, 29 U.S.C. § 794 ('Section 504') and the Americans with Disabilities Act, 42 U.S.C. § 12132 ('ADA'). Appellants alleged that the School District failed to accommodate M.S.'s disabilities and retaliated against her family for asserting their Section 504 and ADA rights. The District Court dismissed the Complaint with prejudice for lack of subject matter jurisdiction because Appellants failed to exhaust their administrative remedies under the Individuals with Disabilities Education Act, 20 U.S.C. §§1400-1482 ('IDEA')."

"Appellants also argue that this case is distinguishable from *Batchelor* because the child in that case had an Individualized Education Plan pursuant to 20 U.S.C. §1414(d) that dictated the terms of his FAPE, while M.S. did not . . . Rather, *Batchelor* makes clear that any plaintiff raising claims that could be remedied through the IDEA's administrative process must exhaust them before filing suit."

"The general rule announced in *Batchelor* is that any non-IDEA claim is subject to the exhaustion requirement if it 'relates to' the 'identification, evaluation, or educational placement of the child, or the provision of a free appropriate public education to such child.'"

BP v. NYC Dept. Ed
2nd Cir. – December 30, 2015

The parents of a child with autism requested reimbursement for private education expenses. Issues included appropriateness of the proposed placement, whether the placement school was able to implement the child's IEP when school staff advised parents otherwise.

The parents "contend that the district court erred in upholding the state review officer's ("SRO") decision not to address the appropriateness of the school placement offered to S.H. The Appeals Court held that the "... district court was not precluded from considering the appropriateness of the placement offered to S.H. solely because S.H. never attended the school."

The parents took issue "... with information provided during their tour of the placement school, and contend that DOE should be estopped from remedying faulty information given to parents through subsequent testimony.

Testimony by the school at the due process hearing was sufficient to refute parents' allegations of representations concerning proposed public placement's inability to implement related services provided in the IEP.

"Here, the record sufficiently demonstrates that the placement school had the ability to implement fully S.H.'s IEP, despite any misinformation provided to plaintiffs. For instance, plaintiffs complain that they were told that the placement school did not have the requisite staffing or space to provide S.H. with the 'pullout' occupational therapy required by his IEP. DOE, however, adduced testimony that the placement school had two occupational therapists available five days a week, who could provide therapy in a service suite where each had his or her own desk ... The same conclusion obtains with respect to IEP-mandated 'pull-out' speech therapy.

"To the extent there was conflicting testimony from B.P. and the social worker who served as plaintiffs' placement school tour guide as to what information was relayed on the tour, the initial hearing officer ('IHO') was in the best position to assess credibility, which he did in favor of the social worker."

"We identify no error in the district court's decision to not address six claims that plaintiffs failed expressly to raise in their due process complaint. See 20 U.S.C. § 1415(f)(3)(B) (stating that party requesting due process hearing shall not be allowed to raise issues at hearing that were not raised in due process complaint unless other party agrees). The due process complaint serves as fair notice to the school district, and gives the district 30 days to resolve the complaint to the parents' satisfaction before a hearing."

" ... plaintiffs claim that 'most of the issues that the SRO precluded, and that the District Court affirmed, were directly referenced in Plaintiffs' letter of July 9, which was cross-referenced in their Due Process complaint. As the district court recognized, however, plaintiffs' letter is referenced in the due process complaint primarily 'as part of [a] chronology of events,' not as an issue requiring resolution."

AL v. Jackson Co. Sch. Bd.
11th Cir. - December 30, 2015

In this Florida case, the child, A.L., "suffers from a traumatic brain injury" and received special education services. The mother requested a due process hearing alleging "that the Board violated the IDEA by (1) failing to include her in a November 17, 2010, IEP development meeting; (2) failing to meet her demand to provide A.L. with an independent educational evaluation; and (3) failing to provide A.L. with special-education services during the summer months."

Other allegations were raised such as a violation of the Fourth Amendment of the U.S. Constitution regarding illegal searches of the youngster and other Section 504 and ADA claims.

"A six-week hearing before the ALJ commenced in September 2011 and concluded in April 2012. By the time the hearing was completed, the ALJ had heard from over 60 witnesses and received more than 160 exhibits. The ALJ entered a lengthy final order on December 27, 2012, denying all of P.L.B.'s claims. As a result of the denial of her claims, P.L.B. filed a complaint in the Northern District of Florida on March 27, 2013. "

The school board filed a Motion for Summary Judgment on all claims, and, after extensions of time were granted, on "October 30, 2014, the district court granted summary judgment to the Board on all counts."

The mother and son appealed to the Eleventh Circuit. That Court noted that we "affirm the district court's entry of summary judgment in favor of the Board on Appellants' IDEA claims and their Section 504 and ADA claims. We reverse and remand for further proceedings on the Fourth Amendment claim."

With regard to claim # 1 about holding the IEP meeting without parent being present, the Court noted that "Although P.L.B. did not explicitly refuse to attend the November 17, 2010, IEP meeting, her actions were tantamount to refusal. The Board attempted to schedule the IEP meeting over several months, with notification to P.L.B. so that she could participate in the process. The attempts to schedule a meeting for the development of A.L.'s IEP began in early August 2010 and continued through mid-November . . . despite the Board's efforts to accommodate P.L.B.'s schedule and demands, P.L.B. either missed or refused to consent to attending four separately scheduled meetings, including the last one, scheduled for November 17, 2010. The Board offered to allow P.L.B. to attend the IEP meeting by telephone, as she had done in the past. P.L.B. refused."

With regard to claim # 2 regarding the Independent Educational Evaluation, the Court explained that "In the spring of 2009, P.L.B. requested an IEE at the Board's expense. When P.L.B. finally chose an evaluator, his fee was $1,500 more than the approved fee. Nonetheless, the Board agreed to cover the fee. Then P.L.B. insisted that the evaluation be conducted by a different evaluator at the Morris Center, a facility 200 miles away. The Board

declined that demand, noting the high expense and the availability of closer, appropriate facilities. Although P.L.B. relented and agreed to have the IEE performed by an evaluator located closer, she did not have the evaluation done. Instead, more than two years later, during the summer of 2012, P.L.B. took her son to Colorado to be evaluated by a doctor from the Morris Center who had since moved."

"Under these circumstances, the Board did not deny Appellants an IEE. Rather, we concur with the well-reasoned decision of the ALJ, as adopted by the district court, that P.L.B.'s actions sabotaged the IEE process."

With regard to claim # 3 regarding ESY "because the school did not offer a regular school environment," the Court explained that "[i]n order to comply with the least-restrictive-environment requirement for the ESY, a school district must consider an appropriate continuum of alternative placements, then must offer the student the least restrictive placement from that continuum that is appropriate for the student's disabilities. The IDEA does not require a school board to create a mainstream summer program to serve the needs of one disabled student . . . [and it does not] require public school districts to create any new ESY programs that they do not currently operate. It is entirely up to each state and each school district to decide how it will fulfill the IDEA's [least restrictive environment] requirement."

The parent also raised as an issue the ESY placement conducting illegal searches of the child in violation of the Fourth Amendment. The teacher patted each child down as he entered the classroom. The Court noted that the school board is required "to show either that A.L. was not searched at all or that he was searched but the search was justified . . ." Because the District Court did not justify searching children as they entered, the Court of Appeals remanded the case to the District Court on that issue.

This page intentionally left blank.

Chapter 4. Legal Research & Tutorial on Google Scholar

In Chapter 1, you learned that when you are researching a legal issue, you need to study the United States Code, the Federal and State Regulations, the *Commentary*, and judicial decisions, i.e., case law on your issue.

If you know a case was appealed, you need to read the earlier decisions that were appealed and reversed, or appealed and affirmed. When you read earlier decisions, you will have a clearer sense about how the law on your issue is evolving.

Chapter 3 contains a Table of Decisions in IDEA Cases by Courts of Appeals in 2015 (begins at page 42). After the Table of Decisions are summaries of each decision. The Table of Decisions includes links to the full text of the decisions from Google Scholar.

Tutorial: Using Google Scholar

When you use Google Scholar, you can search published opinions of state appellate and supreme courts since 1950, opinions from federal district, appellate, tax and bankruptcy courts since 1923, and decisions from the U.S. Supreme Court since 1791.[98]

Google Scholar embeds clickable citation links within cases. The "How Cited" tab retrieves subsequent citations to a particular decision.

Google Scholar also searches peer-reviewed papers, theses, books, preprints, abstracts and technical reports from academic publishers, professional societies, preprint repositories and universities, and scholarly articles available on the Internet.

Let's search for a case listed in the Table of Cases – *Capistrano*.

---

[98] https://en.wikipedia.org/wiki/Google_Scholar Retrieved on February 25, 2016.

First, go to: http://scholar.google.com

Figure 1. Google Scholar Search page.

Click "Case law" (below the Google search box) then click "Select courts ..."

When the "Select courts" page opens, you will see "Federal Courts" on the right side of the page. Go to the 9th Circuit and select "Court of Appeals."

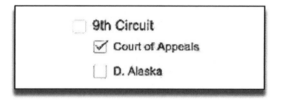

Figure 2. Court of Appeals for the 9th Circuit

Scroll to the bottom of the page and click "Done." A new screen will open that will tell you to: "Please enter a query in the search box above." Insert this term exactly with quotation marks "individuals with disabilities education act"

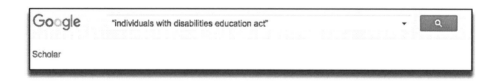

Figure 3. Search for "individuals with disabilities education act"

Add the year - 2015 in this exercise. Add part of the case name, "Capistrano." Your query should now read:

"individuals with disabilities education act" capistrano 2015

Google Scholar will do a full text search of their legal database for all cases from the Court of Appeals for the Ninth Circuit with the words in your query.

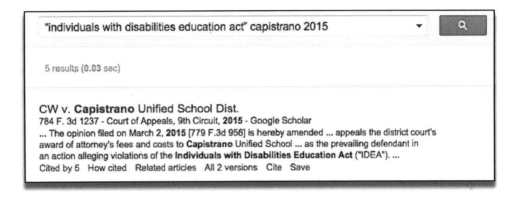

Figure 4. Search for "individuals with disabilities education act" capistrano 2015

You see that *C.W. v. Capistrano Unified School District* was issued on March 2, 2015 and is published at 779 F.3d 996.

You also find *Sam K.*, another case from the 9th Circuit that refers to the *Capistrano* case.

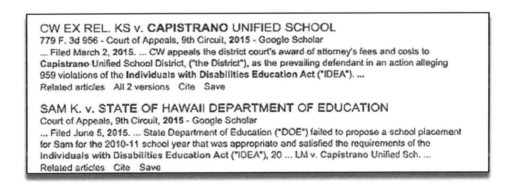

Figure 5. Search Results for *Capistrano.*

When Google Scholar provides you with a long list of cases, you can have the program re-sort the cases into chronological order. By default, Google Scholar will put the most recent case first in the list and provide you with the number of days that have passed since the decision was rendered.

As noted earlier, some cases in ***Wrightslaw: Special Education Legal Developments and Cases 2015*** do not have an F.3d citation. When you find a case on Google Scholar, click the "How Cited" tab on the upper left side of the page to see if the F.3d citation is available now.

Let's try another exercise with Google Scholar.

Change your search query to find cases about an issue that is interests you - dyslexia, autism, Section 504, restraint, damages, retaliation, individualized education program (IEP), independent educational evaluation (IEE), Americans with Disabilities Act (ADA), etc.

Select the U.S. District Courts in your state and your Court of Appeals. Search for cases on your issue.

Next, broaden your search to include cases on your issue from other Circuits. Return to the Courts page and change your Court selections to also include all Courts of Appeals.

You can even search for the name of an individual, an administrator, an expert witness, a Judge, a particular school or school district.

Troubleshooting

On occasion, you may search for a case and not be able to find it. When the authors were creating the database of Court of Appeals cases for ***Wrightslaw: Special Education Legal Developments and Cases 2015,*** we knew about decisions that did not appear when we used the term "Individuals with Disabilities Education Act" in our search. We were perplexed.

When we experimented with search terms, we found these cases. In one instance, the decision had a line break inside the word "Education." The word printed as "Educa-tion" so the Google Scholar search engine did not find it.

Two decisions from the Ninth Circuit referenced IDEA as the "Individuals with Disabilities Education Improvement Act." When we changed our search term to "Individuals with Disabilities Education Improvement Act," we found those two decisions that did not show up in our original search.

On April 1, 2016, we conducted an experiment. We used the term "individuals with disabilities education act" 2016 to search all Courts of Appeals. Google Scholar found 23 cases. We repeated the same search but eliminated the quotation marks. The search was for cases that contained those words, without regard for the order of the words. Google Scholar found 358 cases.

Create a Google Scholar Alert

Go back to your original search page.

At the bottom of the page, you will see a link to "Create alert." When you create an alert, Google Scholar will send you an email alert whenever a decision is issued in the legal jurisdiction you select.

Return to the "Select courts" page. Select the Courts of Appeals for all Circuits, all U.S. District Courts in your State, and all your state courts. Change your search query to "Individuals with Disabilities Education Act" 2016.

Google will notify you of all new IDEA decisions from your federal and state courts and from all Courts of Appeal around the country in 2016.

Figure 6. Create an Alert

In this chapter, you learned how to use Google Scholar to search for legal decisions. You learned how to expand and narrow your search and how to create a Google Alert.

In Summation

In the Introduction to **_Wrightslaw Special Education Legal Developments and Cases 2015,_** we explained why this book is unique. You have special education news, trends and developments in special education law, cases from the Courts of Appeals, and our thoughts about how the law is evolving.

We may publish similar books about legal news, developments and cases annually. We appreciate your thoughts about how we can make these books better. If you wish to share your thoughts by email, please contact us at annual | at | wrightslaw.com (replacing the | at | sign with @).

Or you may write to us at:

Pete & Pam Wright / Wrightslaw Year in Review
c/o Harbor House Law Press, Inc.
P.O. Box 480
Hartfield, VA 23071

Thank you!

Pete and Pam Wright

About the Authors

Pete Wright is an attorney who represents children with special educational needs. Pete struggled with learning disabilities, including dyslexia, dysgraphia and ADHD. His determination to help children grew out of his own educational experiences.

Pam Wright is a psychotherapist who has worked with children and families since the 1970's. Her training and experience in clinical psychology and clinical social work give her a unique perspective on parent-child-school dynamics, problems and solutions. Pam has written extensively about raising, educating, and advocating for children with disabilities.

The Wrights provide accurate, up-to-date information about special education law, education law, and advocacy for children with disabilities at Wrightslaw.com, the #1 ranked special education website.

Wrightslaw began in 1993, when Pete Wright argued Shannon Carter's case before The U. S. Supreme Court. The Supreme Court issued a unanimous decision on Shannon's behalf in *Florence County School District Four v. Shannon Carter,* 510 U.S. 7, (1993).

Each year, Pete and Pam Wright present Wrightslaw Special Education Law and Advocacy Training Programs around the country. The Wrightslaw Speakers Bureau includes other nationally-recognized experts in the field of special education law and advocacy.

Pete and Pam Wright were Adjunct Professors of Law at the William and Mary School of Law where they taught a course about special education law and assisted with creation of the PELE Special Education Law Clinic. Pete and Pam are co-founders and faculty at the William & Mary Law Institute of Special Education Advocacy (ISEA).

Pete and Pam Wright live on Stingray Point, Deltaville, Virginia. They sail, windsurf, fish, kayak, explore, and have adventures.

Books, Training Downloads, DVDs & Websites

Wrightslaw is an important part of our identity so we include **"Wrightslaw"** in the titles of our books that are available in the Wrightslaw Store at www.wrightslaw.com/store.

Pete and Pam Wright are co-authors of several books, including:

Wrightslaw: From Emotions to Advocacy, 2nd Edition (2006)

Wrightslaw: Special Education Law, 2nd Edition (2007)

Wrightslaw: All About IEPs (2010)

Wrightslaw: All About Tests and Assessments (2014)

DVD Video: *Wrightslaw: Surviving Due Process: Stephen Jeffers v. School Board* - award-winning documentary (2 hours).

Multimedia Training Programs: Understanding Your Childs Test Scores (1.5 hours) and Wrightslaw Special Education Law and Advocacy Training (6.5 hours).

Pete and Pam built several websites to help parents of children with disabilities in their quest for quality special education programs.

Fetaweb.com, the companion website to *Wrightslaw: From Emotions to Advocacy*, has advocacy information and resources to supplement the book. http://www.fetaweb.com

IDEA 2004 at Wrightslaw provides current information about the Individuals with Disabilities Education Act of 2004 (IDEA 2004). http://www.wrightslaw.com/idea/index.htm

The **Yellow Pages for Kids with Disabilities** includes a directory of educational consultants, advocates, advisors, psychologists, diagnosticians, health care specialists, tutors, speech language therapists, and attorneys by state. You'll also find links to government programs, your State Department of Education websites, special education regulations, grassroots organizations, disability organizations, legal and advocacy resources, special education schools, and parent support groups. http://www.yellowpagesforkids.com

We invite you to join our online community on the **Wrightslaw Way Blog** at http://www.wrightslaw.com/blog

Index

63550989R00060

Made in the USA
Lexington, KY
10 May 2017